PALMISTRY

PALMISTRY

THE PRACTICE OF HAND READING

JOHNNY FINCHAM

SIRIUS

Hand illustrations: Copyright © Arcturus Publishing Ltd.
Additional images courtesy of Shutterstock.

SIRIUS

This edition published in 2024 by Sirius Publishing, a division of
Arcturus Publishing Limited,
26/27 Bickels Yard, 151–153 Bermondsey Street,
London SE1 3HA

ISBN: 978-1-3988-3606-8
AD011468UK

Printed in China

CONTENTS

Introduction **6**

History of Palmistry. **8**

1 Getting Started **11**

Equipment 12

Guidelines on Getting Started 14

The Modern Approach 16

2 The Different Palms **19**

3 The Fingers **35**

4 Print Patterns **61**

5 Palmer Patterns **79**

6 Major Lines **91**

7 Minor Lines .117

8 How to Give a Palm Reading **155**

9 Palmistry at a Professional Level **177**

Quick Reference List **196**

Further Reading **204**

Introduction

Why on earth would anyone in the modern world want to study an archaic art like palmistry?

Well, the answer is easy – palmistry has much to teach us. Probably the true power of palmistry is only now beginning to be realized as a massively insightful tool for self-understanding.

You can forget any lingering superstitions you may have, like a short lifeline predicting an early death; these old meanings are nonsense. Far from scanning for mystic signs like the 'sacred cross' and making predictions, we palm readers have a view into human nature that can give people invaluable insight into their lives and their inner being.

In the contemporary times we live in, we're presented with a bewildering set of options, and we can so easily get sucked up into becoming someone we aren't. The pressure of social media is particularly pervasive, dragging us away from our true natures. Knowing ourselves though our palms is a fundamental pathway to free us from making poor personal decisions and evolving into our true selves.

Only a little way down the road as a beginner palm reader, you can ascertain a person's sensitivity,

confidence, sense of security, competitiveness, emotional warmth and a thousand other qualities. Much can be learned from the palm in a few minutes that might take a person half a lifetime to work out. All your flaws, patterns and qualities are marked in your palm and, with a little patience, you will soon learn how to interpret anyone's hand. The palm is a map of the deeper personality and all is drawn there for those that can read the signs. This book will teach you all you need to know. Go gently into the practice; take time to absorb each sign and indication as you go. Once you start to apply your knowledge you will be astonished at how penetrating, true and insightful palm reading can be. The journey starts here. Let's go!

History of Palmistry

Palmistry is one of the most ancient practices known to mankind. In almost every early civilisation, some form of palmistry was practised. The ancient Chinese, Babylonians, Greeks and Romans all studied palmistry. The earliest written reference to palm reading is in the Vedas, the sacred texts of the Indus Valley which date back over 6000 years. Palmistry is referenced by Aristotle in his text *Historia Animalium* (361BCE) and palmistry is mentioned three times in the Bible.

Throughout most of its history, palmistry was one of many forms of divination used to predict the future and to warn people of what fate, destiny or karma had in store for them. The lines of the hands were believed to remain unchanged and fixed throughout one's lifetime. Signs like the 'mystic cross', 'star of fortune', 'sacred triangle' and other such formations in the lines of the hand took on enormous importance as indications of good (or bad) omens.

In the past 70 years or so, however, palmistry has evolved enormously as a growing body of evidence from scientists, anthropologists, medical researchers and others have had a massive influence on the way palm readers view the hand. We now see the palm as a 'window' onto the personality, rather than as a predictive tool.

CHAPTER ONE

Getting Started

Equipment

Magnifying glass

The most important piece of equipment you need is a magnifying glass. It's important, because you can't see the fine palmer lines nor identify the print patterns without one. Try to get a glass with a lens around 10cm across. Ideally it will have a light built-in, so you can see detail in poor light. A magnification of somewhere around x3 is plenty, but do make sure you can easily make out your fingerprints under the glass before you buy it.

Some readers read from the flesh-and-blood palm and some take a set of prints to work from.

If using the print-taking method, you'll need:

- block printing, water-based ink

- an ink roller

- plain A4 photocopying paper

To take an ink impression, first squeeze a small amount of ink onto a smooth surface and roll the roller over it until it's covered in a fine, thin layer. Then roll the roller all over the palm and fingers, coating them in just enough ink to highlight all the lines and prints. If you put too much ink on it will 'flood' the lines and make them hard to make out.

Place a newspaper under the print paper and press the inked palm down onto the paper with firm pressure, using both your hands. Then lift the hand off carefully, holding the printed paper down with one hand while you do so.

You will probably need to practice with six or so sets of prints before you get them to come out just right.

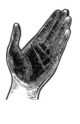
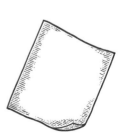

Guidelines on Getting Started

Like any practice, palmistry has its own set of rules to work by. Take time to memorize these principles, as they will make both study and practice much easier. The fundamental precepts of palmists are known as the 'rules of thumb'.

The five rules of thumb

1. Tempting though it is to jump in and highlight that amazing head line, or island on the heart line, you need to take your time and build a picture of your client in your mind before you start to talk. You must take *all the points* from *both hands* into account. So don't rush, be patient, and work carefully through every significant point before you make any comments. No single observation can be seen in isolation, it must be balanced with everything else you see in the hands.

2. *If any digit, line, mount or marking is common and normal, ignore it. You are only always looking for points that make a person individual and distinct from everyone else. No-one wants to know how ordinary they are!*

3. Understand that the lines of the palm change through time, people change, grow and develop and what is marked in the lines now, may not be there next month, next year or in ten years.

4. There is a positive and negative aspect to every feature on the palm. No exceptions.

5. Palmistry is a caring profession, it is not about impressing people or frightening them. Try always to be diplomatic, gentle and supportive to the person you're reading for. A palm reading can often open up massive issues in a person's life and you need to be sensitive to this. It will be necessary to acquire some basic counselling skills.

The Modern Approach

A massive step forward in the way palmists work came with the publication in 1951 of *The hand in psychological diagnosis* by mental health physician and psychoanalyst, Charlotte Wolff. This book showed many examples of the hands of people with serious genetic learning difficulties, demonstrating a link between brain development and hand development. In more recent years, scientific research has linked relative finger length and fingerprint patterns with distinct character traits, expanding our understanding of the hand considerably further.

This has meant that from a palm reader's perspective, the best way to view the palm is a kind of porthole that allows one to see into the workings of the brain. In terms of anthropological development, there's a well-established link between the way the human hand has become increasingly sophisticated and the way the human brain has evolved. A massive amount of the cerebral cortex is devoted to the palms. In proportion to the amount of brain surface area given to, for example, the knees, the palm's brain allocation is for a pair of organs each around the size of a car's windscreen!

When you look at a person's hands, try to imagine you're looking into the mind of that person, seeing the flexibility, sensitivity, amount of reasoning power, emotionality and all the other qualities that make a human being.

The palm itself (without the digits) is representative of the old mammalian primal part of the brain, which deals with the need for shelter, food, survival and maintenance of all the bodily processes.

The digits are representative of the more modern, evolved brain, where we process information about social status, communication, sense of self, values, our place in society and so on.

CHAPTER TWO

THE DIFFERENT PALMS

Active and Passive Hands

So, which palm is the one to examine? The right or the left? Well, you need to scrutinize both hands, whether the person you're reading for is left- or right-handed, old or young, male, female or non-binary. The hand you catch a ball with (the right on most people) is termed the active hand while the one you use less (usually the left) is called the passive hand.

Some people are ambidextrous (equally adept with both palms) and in this case the hand with the stiffest thumb should be termed the active.

Old-fashioned palmistry books will tell you the passive hand shows a person's past and the active hand is where their future lies, but this is simply not true. We are always to some extent using both hands (and using both hemispheres of our brains).

The active hand shows the more outwardly-focused, developed, expressive, mature personality and the passive palm shows the deeper, hidden, immature, personal and private personality. Both palms are indicative of how you are now, but everyone has a deeper side of their personality that's usually hidden. The active and passive hands are akin to the difference between meeting a person at work (their active hand), when they are operating fully conscious and displaying their social face, and living with a partner for ten years whom you know very well (their passive hand). Your knowledge of their deeper self means you are aware they daydream a lot, curl into a ball during thunderstorms and are prone to weep at romantic films.

The differences between the active and passive palms are crucial in hand analysis. There might be, for instance, insecurity (shown by a broken lifeline) in the passive palm and this might drive the ambition (shown by a set of aspiration lines) in the active hand. Seeing oppositional patterns in the palms can tell you a lot about what motivates a person and where they might get pulled by contradictory impulses.

Children are much more open and undeveloped than adults and their passive palms reflect the personality more strongly. It's fascinating to watch the lines on children's palm develop as their brains develop. Children's palms shift and change their line formation much quicker than adults. After puberty, the active hand becomes the dominant one and reflects more accurately the outer person.

Palm Shape

In palmistry the first step in analysis is to establish the overall shape of the palm.

Hands fall into four rough categories – square palms with short fingers – square palms with long fingers, rectangular palms with short fingers and narrow rectangular palms with long fingers.

We allocate a different element to each shape and at the most fundamental level, the hand shape reflects the instinctive personality.

It can take some time to recognise the elemental shapes, so give yourself a little while to work this out. Start with your own hand, and go from there.

Some people (around a quarter of the population) have undefined palms, which don't fall into a particular category. In this case, simply ignore the hand shape and go to the next step.

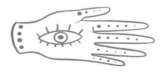

EARTH HANDS

Square palms with short fingers

Earth hands have short fingers with large, square, heavy palms. The bones of the palm are thick and the digits usually stiff. The palm dominates the digits, so the Earth personality is dominated by the physical, sensual and practical things in life.

The Earth person tends to have a short, stocky body shape and they tend to be physically strong, robust, slow to react and down-to-earth. The short fingers and broad palm show a dislike of abstract ideas; they would much rather be doing something than sitting around thinking.

Earth people have natural manual skills and they are found in all the professions where practical skills are important – hairdressing, horticulture, tradespeople, cooks, cleaners, farmers and mechanics.

The Earth type is cautious, home- and family-loving and highly security conscious. They are unpretentious, grounded and nature-loving and invariably have large families with lots of pets.

Earth is beneath our feet and easily taken for granted. So often Earth people do essential work, like growing food or building houses – all the vital maintenance that keeps life going – yet they are often beneath our notice and unappreciated.

AIR HANDS
Square palms, long fingers
The opposite to Earth is Air. Air hands are large but light in weight, with thin, bird-like bones and long fingers. Air people are usually tall and slim. The square palm gives a practical framework, but the long fingers make for a person that dwells a great deal in the abstract, airy realm. Air types can be very distant, often flying off somewhere in their minds, or drifting into daydream and speculation. The Air type loves to think, talk, teach and learn and all the world of the media – writing, broadcasting, publishing, teaching and entertaining – is dominated by Air-handed people. They have an adherence to principles, values, ethics and ideas, often failing to deal with practical problems because it conflicts with a value system or ideal. Air people are found in any area of life where they can work independently and non-manually. Air types are often highly educated and, though often

very knowledgable and intelligent, their tendency to specialize often makes them poor at dealing with areas outside their own field.

The Air person is usually witty, ironic, somewhat dry and has a keen sense of humour. They often flap their hands in a bird-like manner when talking, throwing ideas around the place.

FIRE HANDS
Rectangular palms, short fingers

Fire hands are the most difficult to identify, as they are a sort of 'middling' hand. The palms are rectangular, but not so narrow as water hands, the fingers are short, but not so short as earth hands.

Where the palms become more narrow, the person is more influenced by their environment. When the digits are short, there is less of an eye for detail, analysis and study. The Fire hand is rectangular, muscular, smallish in size, warm to the touch, with short (often knotty) fingers.

The rectangular palm makes for a highly responsive and adaptable personality who is dynamic, competitive, impatient with detail, and quick to adapt to new trends, movements and skills. Fire types tend to be somewhat frustrated with slower, less ambitious people, as they are always highly motivated and driven. Achieving the goal is the natural tendency and no time is wasted on failure or sentimentality. Risk is an issue for Fire personalities, as they are drawn to adventurous and (often) dangerous sports and occupations, and are great believers in the old adage 'if you don't take risks – you don't drink champagne'.

Fire people are drawn to any situation where glamour, excitement, and drama are found. Usually the body type is slightly on the short side, with well-developed musculature and the eyes are very penetrating. Usually Fire types will stand out in some way by having dramatic hair, dress, tattoos or some other distinction.

WATER HANDS
Narrow rectangular palm, long fingers.

The narrow palm of the Water hand gives a strong capacity to be shaped and moulded by exterior factors. The long fingers give a dreamy, abstract quality to the personality.

Water hands are often pale and cool to the touch, the

fingers are long and flexible and the palm a narrow rectangle. Water-handed people are naturally caring and compassionate as they are highly responsive to the people around them. Their long digits give a fascination with higher emotional realms – dreams, intuition, magic, mystery and the arts. Water-handed people are the least physically robust and the most naturally artistic of the four elements.

This hand type is usually given to having long hair, whatever their gender, and they tend to avoid any type of vocation that cannot employ the emotions in some way. They are very drawn to working with children, animals, nursing, alternative therapies and to art of all kinds.

The body tends to be very flexible and they can gain weight very easily. Often enigmatic and with a fluid, sensuous way of moving, the Water person is fascinated by relationships, feelings, the inner world and romanticism. There can be a tendency to self-absorption and moodiness, and they can easily find they are moved, motivated and shaped by the people, situations and environment they find themselves in.

Skin Texture

The skin on the inner palm is enormously important in palmistry. We know that the hands contain some of the densest areas of nerve endings in the body and are the richest source of tactile feedback. The skin on the surface of the palm and fingertips is made up lines of papillary ridges that are infused with a network of special receptors.

There is a great variety in skin ridge texture. The more tightly the skin ridges are packed together, the more sensitive the person is. When the skin on the hand is very hard and rough, with well-spread, crude skin ridges, the more impervious the person is to heat, pain, awareness of atmosphere, etc. Of course, manual work will create hard calluses of skin on the palms. However, this won't affect the basic skin ridge density.

As a palmist, you need to develop a 'feel' for the skin texture by running your index finger over the inner palm of a range of very different people with varying palmer skin. This can only be developed by getting lots of experience, but you can kick-start your ability to judge skin quality by finding a silk-skinned hand of someone who you know is very sensitive and gentle and highly aware, and compare that to the skin texture of someone you know who spends all their time outdoors, is extremely hardy and impervious to the weather and who is very 'thick-skinned' in terms of sensitivity.

Always check the skin by stroking with the index finger of your right hand (the most sensitive fingertip) over an area in the centre of the palm where there are no calluses.

Palmists divide the skin on the inner palm into four categories based on degree of sensitivity. The most rough and hard is 'coarse' skin, next comes 'grainy' skin, then 'paper' skin and lastly, the most fine and sensitive - 'silk' skin.

Be careful when you judge the skin of the very elderly - those in their eighties and beyond tend to have very, very fine skin on the inner palm - this is a marker of the skin becoming very thin in old age, and it is much harder to judge the skin texture.

Silk

When the skin on the inner palm is very fine, silky, soft, and the skin ridges so densely packed you can't feel them at all, you have a person with silk skin. There are many, many, fine scratchy lines all over the palm.

Silk skin makes for an extremely sensitive constitution, someone highly aware of atmosphere, touch, temperature and other's moods. Men with silk skin often struggle to express a traditionally masculine role in life. Intuitive and sensitive, silk-skinned people try to avoid competition and harsh environments and are prone to allergies. They appreciate finesse and luxury, and have a delicate palate.

Paper

Skin that's fine, dry and often slightly yellowish where you can just perceive the skin ridges is paper skin. There are usually quite a number of lines on the palm.

This skin quality is common. It creates a responsiveness to visual and verbal stimuli. This type of palm touches paper, books, computers, phones and connects to others through the mass of media networks. Paper skin people can sometimes be a little dry and distant and sometimes are wary of physical touch.

Grainy

Grainy skin has ridges that are clearly visible and easily felt. The lines on the palm are deep, red and easily seen, like cuts. Usually the palm has a slightly hard feel to it. This type of palm is made to do, act, initiate and work. Such skin is always found on busy people. This is someone restless and active, who's always working and not particularly inward-looking or reflective. They're very often also sporty and business-minded.

Coarse

Coarse skin is immediately obvious. The palm feels very hard and very rough, there are very few lines and the lines are deep, trough-like grooves. Coarse-skinned people love to be outdoors and to touch brick, steel, wood and dirt. This skin type is abrasive in nature and found on builders, farmers, fishermen and outdoor workers in general. These people hate to be confined to a centrally-heated office and need to be physically active. They are incredibly hardy and resilient, but not at all subtle, intuitive or sensitive to other's feelings.

CHAPTER THREE

THE FINGERS

The Fingers

When you examine the fingers, you're bound to find something really interesting. Either in the length, stiffness or print pattern, the fingers identify powerful character traits, the manner of thinking and deep issues developed from the kind of upbringing a person has had.

It's very important to be diplomatic and sensitive when you explore the qualities of the digits.

Where the body of the palm represents the primal, instinctive brain, the fingers indicate the modern, highly developed parts of the brain for ego, persona, status, conformity, speech and other qualities that give us the ability to function in modern, complex societies.

The finger's relative growth and development is dependent on hormonal exposure in the womb, and to childhood conditioning. The fingers aren't really fully formed until after puberty. Until the late teens, the finger balance can still change.

The qualities that need to be checked when examining the digits and thumbs are their length in relationship to each other, their stiffness and the print patterns.

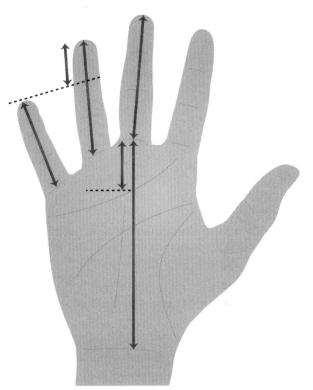

Flexibility

Stiffness of the fingers is checked by simply placing your palm against the fingertips of the hand of the person you're reading for and gently pushing the all the digits back toward the wrist.

As you know, we ignore the average, so if the fingers pull back two or three inches, this is normal and of no consequence.

Finger flexibility is mental flexibility. Fingers which hardly move back when you push against them show high internal stress, rigid mental processes and a lack of spontaneity. This can be positive in an area of life where conformity and rigid mind-sets are important, like the military.

Where the fingers are floppy and bend back 45 degrees or more, it shows an impulsive mind. Open, spontaneous and expressive, this is a person receptive to new ideas but psychologically all over the place, never sticking to any view, value or opinion for long. Flexible digits are normal on children's hands, and common on the hands of artists and dancers.

Standard Finger Length

When you find a finger shorter or longer than average, it's enormously important. It indicates the particular way a person has adapted psychologically and shows their evolvement of the sense of self (index), attitude to society (middle finger), drive for status (ring digit) and capacity for speech (little finger). The fingers are highly revealing about childhood and the way a person has been brought up. Whenever a digit is extra long or short, it will manifest on both active and passive hands.

In palmistry we traditionally used the planets to describe the qualities of each finger. However, this system originated when astrology was the basis for medicine, chemistry, physics and philosophy. In contemporary language, planetary description is mostly meaningless.

Modern palm readers use metaphors for the fingers to make their qualities easy to understand. The metaphors we use are: the *mirror finger* of self-consciousness, pride and power issues for the index finger (by far the most important digit);

the *wall* finger of boundaries, values, conformity and normality for the middle digit; the *peacock* of persona, self-expression, performance and kudos for the ring finger; and the *antenna* digit of sexual, signal and verbal communication for the little finger.

In order to work out which digits are unusually long or short on anyone's palm, you need to know the standard, average relative finger lengths. Bear in mind that it's very common for anyone to have at least one finger extra long, extra short or bent.

Normally, the index and ring fingers are almost the same length, with the ring finger just slightly longer (only 1 or 2 millimetres) than the index. If the index looks the same length as the ring digit, or is the just the slightest fraction longer, it's considered a long mirror finger and if more than 2mm shorter, it's considered short.

The middle digit normally has almost half the top phalange jutting above a line drawn across the top of the ring and index digits. This one is the hardest to judge, and needs a little experience of seeing an extra long and a seriously short finger be able to judge correctly.

The little finger normally comes up to the second (higher) crease line of the ring finger.

You can easily check index and ring finger length by running a ruler across the tip of these two digits, pushing the middle finger back. If the ruler's level, the fingers are the same length and the index must be considered long. If it drops in either direction you can easily see which one is the longer. Remember, if the index is just 2mm shorter, this is normal and can be disregarded.

Draw a line with a pen along the straight edge where it crosses the middle finger, then you can easily establish an average and where the middle finger's long or short.

The little finger is easily checked by seeing if it reaches to the top crease of the ring finger, if longer than this, it's long, if the tip is some way below this point, it's short.

The Thumb

The thumb is expressive of the will, self-control and drive a person has. The key qualities of the thumb are its stiffness and length. If you look at the thumbs of those with tremendous self-discipline, like Olympic athletes and professional footballers, you'll always see a long, very stiff thumb.

To check flexibility of the thumb, push it back towards the wrist. It will always be a little stiffer on the active hand. Most thumbs move back half an inch or so and this is the unremarkable average. When the thumb bends back almost to the wrist, it's a flexible thumb. When it won't bend back at all, it's a stiff thumb.

Floppy-thumbed folk are easygoing, laid-back people. They're found on those that work at doing things they enjoy. They're particularly common in the arts and on those that work in sociable, leisure and pleasure vocations. However, they hate pushing themselves too hard.

Stiff-thumbed people are stiff in their resolve. They tend to stick to a course of action once it's decided. They're persistent and stick to their goals without bending over backward for anyone else.

The length of the thumb is measured by laying it against the base of the index finger. If the tip comes up to anywhere along the bottom section of the index finger, it's of normal, average length. If it makes it to the first joint line of the mirror finger – it shows huge reserves of will power, great drive and energy and an intolerance of the lazy and unmotivated.

If the thumb doesn't make it to the base of the index finger, it shows someone poor at motivating themselves. Such people easily find themselves 'under the thumb' of gurus, cults, dominant partners and bosses.

Mirror Finger

The mirror finger is all about self reflection. It rules the ego, and is thus the most important digit. Even the slightest bend, length variation or unusual print pattern will make a massive difference to the personality.

This finger rules self-esteem, pride, integrity, responsibility, ambition, sense of power, personal vision and the need for control.

When you find the finger long (even by only a tiny fraction compared to the peacock digit), there's a marked bossiness and a strong need to take control of situations. A long mirror person often takes on high levels of responsibility in any work situation as they are so capable and always exceed expectations.

This is a classic sign of an ambitious perfectionist who finds failure difficult and who has a strong sense of their own worth.

This digit is about the mother relationship when growing up. When long it means childhood was marked by a precocious over-awareness of self, early maturity, and a high sense of responsibility. This is usually the result of a mother figure who abdicated her role which the child had to fill or a super-strong mother who pushed adulthood onto the child's shoulders at an early age.

When this digit is short, it's been linked in many scientific studies to poor self-esteem, lack of a sense of personal power, and poor life choices. There is fear of great responsibility and a lack of self examination.

short

It indicates a childhood where personal power and responsibility was poorly enforced. This is usually because of neglect or by having 'helicopter' parents absolving the need to grow, mature, and face the realities of life. A short mirror finger is an indicator that a person can be dominated in their personal life by a stronger (longer mirror-fingered) personality.

long

When this finger bends, it is always in the direction of the neighbouring wall finger. It shows a need to conform and to belong to the hierarchy of the family, company, tradition or country. Often this sign is found on the dependable manager or team leader in an organization—someone who lacks the straight-up character to be the boss.

average

Wall Finger

This is the longest digit, because it rules all those invisible qualities we absorb that enable us to find a place in society: stability, vocation, codes of behaviour, religion, balance, boundaries, norms and sense of belonging to a nation, tribe, group or family.

When this finger is short, it shows that the values and norms of family and society have been rejected at some level and this person struggles to belong. It may be because the parents were fanatically religious or rigid in their rules, or they may have been strongly alternative. Either way, the child has rejected life as exemplified by their parents. The short wall can, ironically appear on the headteacher, or prison guard who is drawn to a life with fixed boundaries and rules because they lacked any during childhood. More commonly though, the short wall finger is found on all those that embrace alternative cultures – vegans, animal rightists, communists, anarchists – those who want to challenge the rules, boundaries and status quo. Where this sign used to be rare, it is now common and must be a reflection on the way modern society is changing.

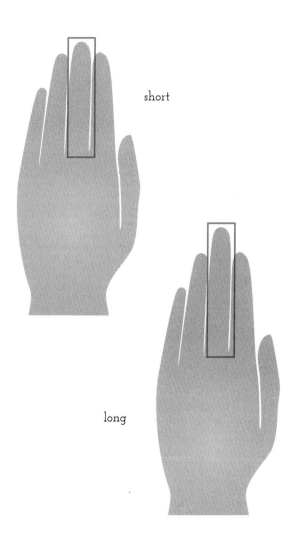

short

long

In some very old palmistry books, it was noted that the short wall finger was common on those who lived in a country other than that of their birth and this is just as true today.

When the digit is found longer than normal, there's a serious attitude to one's profession, family and religion. This sign is found on those whose work involves intricate and detailed knowledge with lots of qualifications, professional grades and certificates. It always shows a serious side to the character, where duty to society is taken very much to heart. It's common on those in the legal, medical, academic and scientific worlds. A big wall finger is found on those that work in big, institutional buildings, with high walls: mosques, museums, universities, cathedrals, law courts and hospitals.

When the wall finger bends, it's invariably in the direction of the peacock finger. This indicates a skewed sense of values where one is oppressed by the demands of work and family and is therefore desperate to escape the rat-race for a fun-filled, carefree life.

Peacock Finger

This digit is about the public face, the need to be popular, the drive to compete, excel, stand out and be appreciated by others. Psychologically, it's the deep-rooted display instinct in the Darwinian competition to attract a mate. This finger, when long is strongly associated with the arts and with a sense of drama.

When long, there's a strong need for self-expression and to be noticed. This may be a subliminal drive, so may take the form of a writer, prize marrow-grower or other passive form of self-expression. If on a more extroverted personality, then it may take the form of dyed blue hair, lots of tattoos and a huge Facebook following.

The long peacock is found on performers of all kinds, artists, actors, dancers, sportspeople, and so on. Obviously, this finger is only long in comparison with the mirror finger, so the longer it is, the more the sense of self-esteem is diminished as evidenced by a small mirror. However tremendous the talent and ability, there are also deep levels of self-neglect and a sense of inferiority. Sadly, those that burn so brightly are often deeply damaged people, as the litany of self-destructive artists and performers shows all too well.

short

long

Merely having this finger long does not make a person talented, only that there is a strong drive to make oneself outstanding. It is linked to risk-taking and recklessness in the rush to make an impression.

When this digit is short then the need to be respected, pride, personal control, and integrity (mirror finger values) are much more important than simple popularity. It won't inhibit the ability to be creative or artistic, but it will mean that the long mirror finger person will have very strict limits as to how far they will go to be in the public eye.

When the peacock digit bends, it will be in the direction of the wall digit. This means that the person's sense of fun and self-expression is bent towards the demands of duty, work, and family (wall finger issues). It can blunt the drive to be creative as one is always hampered by a too-strong sense of commitment and obligation.

Antenna Finger

The antenna digit is a measure of the neuro-linguistic part of the brain. It is about every level of communication: wit, charm, eloquence, sexuality, language abilities and articulacy.

When the finger is found long, it shows a natural language skills, someone who probably learned to read and write at an early age, a love of words, wit, eloquence and skill with words. A long antenna always

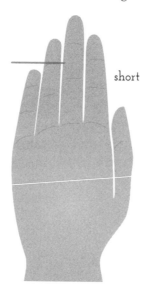

short

shows a sophisticated sexuality and a heightened feel for non-verbal communication. A strong sense of irony is always present. This finger is always found long in those in the fields of publishing, writing, teaching, sales, marketing and the media.

Where this finger's found short, there's a preference to use blunt or direct language. There is suspicion of wordiness, eloquence and wit, as well as a distinct unease with sarcasm and irony. Humour is somewhat obvious and lacking in subtlety.

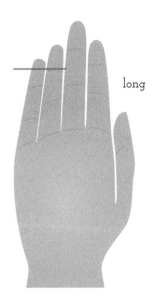

long

All those with a short antenna should be encouraged to gain more confidence with words by reading and writing as much as possible.

Low-set antenna

Children always have a low-set antenna finger. The first crease line on the antenna is initially at the same level as, or lower than, the base of the neighbouring peacock digit. At adolescence, one of the many changes in the body is that this digit is pushed upward so the first crease line is half way up the bottom phalange of the peacock digit. However, on around a quarter of adults, this digit stays low-set. This is thought to be because of an issue with the father figure. A long antenna finger can initially appear short if it's low set in the palm. In such cases, add an imaginary half inch to the tip of the finger to judge it correctly. A low-set antenna is linked to delayed emotional maturity and the need for a replacement father figure. It is a very common pattern found where there is early parenthood with an older partner in women and a tendency to be influenced by a dominant older male in men. Whenever you see this sign, you should advise the low-set antenna person not to rush into marriage, parenthood or reliance on older males. After the age of 30 the emotional maturity finally kicks in and much more appropriate choices are made in relationships.

If the antenna finger bends, it's always inward, toward the peacock digit. This is traditionally the sign of a good liar, who can use words to beguile others. More charitably, it is a signal of someone who has the gift of bending words to give the right effect – a charmer, flatterer or diplomat.

CHAPTER FOUR

PRINT PATTERNS

Brainwaves and Print Patterns

The fingerprints are massively important in modern palmistry. An enormous amount of scientific research has established direct links between specific fingerprint patterns and particular psychological attitudes. The scientific word for the print patterns is dermatoglyphics (from the Greek: *derma*-skin and *glyph*-markings). The prints are formed from the skin ridges which cover the inner palm which we discussed in the chapter on the palm skin types.

The best way to visualize the print patterns is as brainwaves, representing mental processing. Fingerprints help us to see the manner of a person's thinking. We can't know *what* they're thinking, but the prints give us an understanding of the *way* they think.

Of course, every print on every palm is an original and unique marking but all print patterns fall into five broad types. These five patterns are: the simple arch; loop (ulnar and radial); whorl; double loop composite; and tented arch.

Whorl Prints

The whorl print is made of a series of ever-decreasing circles or a spiral which curls into itself. Sometimes there are a few loop lines wrapped around the whorl. The whorl pattern gives a need for space, isolation, privacy and the need to work lone. Whorls on many fingers make for an odd, inventive and highly original personality who's not at all interested in following trends, fashions and groups. The whorl is seen in abundance on creative people. It isn't on it's own a sign of creativity, but it signals a lack of a herd instinct, originality and the ability to be alone for long periods, which is the basis for any individual creative expression. The nature of the whorl means that deep focus on one particular subject is far preferable to a broad, variable set of skills.

Simple Arch Prints

The simple arch is a flat, chevron shape, made of a series of inverted 'V' shaped lines piled on top of each other. The simple arch is a sign of a highly repressed personality; someone fixed, faithful, deep, loyal, dependable, fair-minded and practical. The need to repress emotion can mean it's hard for them to show vulnerability or to let off steam. The simple arch has a powerful drive to protect, defend and save animals, nature, family members and the oppressed. This pattern can give a very good ability to use one's hands, so it's common on craftspeople and those that shape, mould and repair. It's always a sign of someone that will put faith, family and financial security above all other drives.

Tented Arches

These form a distinctive 'spike' formation that lifts high like a tent pole with the lines 'pushed' up around it.

Tented arches are indicators of an intense personality. This marker gives a drive to lift, dramatize, shock and excite. Tented arch people are never boring, they have a powerful drive to push themselves beyond normal boundaries so are highly adventurous, quick-thinking and are highly responsive. This pattern has been linked to heart palpitations, mania and a tendency to over-dramatize, so they need both an exciting outlet for their energies and to learn how to relax.

Loop Prints

By far the most common pattern you'll come across are ulnar loops. Ulnar loops thrown in the direction of the thumb, and they rise and fall like a wave. Sixty-seven per cent of all the prints you'll see are ulnar loops. The loop is about the drive to go with the flow, to respond to others and to have a strong empathy to one's group, family and environment. Group players, band members, actors, people-people all have lots of loops. Generally, loops are seen as the most contented of patterns as it's about fitting in and prioritising friendships and relationships.

Because the ulnar loop is normal and common, we palmists ignore them in a reading.

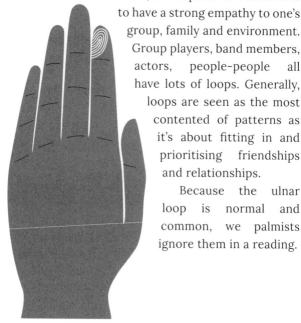

Radial Loop

When you find a loop moving in the *opposite* direction to the common ulna loop, it's known as a radial loop and it's highly significant. It's easy to see the difference as the radial loop moves *away* from the thumb on either hand, hence it's often called by palm readers the 'reversed loop'. The radial loop creates hyper receptivity to the needs of others, and an enormous over-sensitivity to being criticized. It's as if the loop in this direction creates a wave of energy from other people that interferes with one's stability. This pattern is often found on the pleaser, flatterer or enabler. The ideal vocation for the radial loop is some kind of carer, therapist, advisor, PR professional or HR manager. The radial pattern creates a need to be liked.

Composite

The composite is formed by two loops going in opposite directions, like the yin-yang symbol of the Tao. This is considered a spiritual sign in Eastern cultures. The two loops form two waves in opposition to each other and so this pattern is a sign of dualism, doubt, uncertainty and never being able to fully commit. It is a distinctly helpful sign on anyone who is in a position of looking at all sides of any issue and being non-judgemental, like a counsellor, legal representative, academic or advisor.

Where this sign is found there is always going to be a fascination with philosophy and spiritual practice and a natural drive to be non-judgemental.

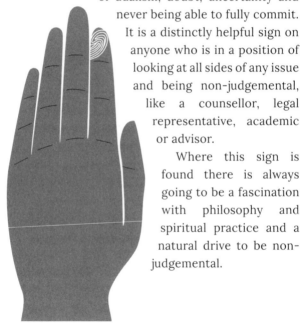

Print Patterns on Individual Fingers

Now that you know the meanings of the print patterns, it's important to understand that the prints only affect the part of the hand (and part of the brain) relating to the area it's found on. The print on the mirror finger is the most important pattern as this is about the way a person processes information about their ego and self-reflection. The print on the wall finger is about your attitude to family, conformity and vocation. The ring finger's print is about your sense of self-expression. The pattern on the antenna indicates the way you process communication skills and sexuality. The thumb's print is about how you use your will and drive to attain goals.

When you examine anyone's hand, always look for differences between the print patterns on the active and passive hands. These show the difference between the underlying and undeveloped character (passive) and the fully developed and expressed character (active). Sometimes the differences are remarkable and there are literally two different characters on the inner and outer selves. This will often indicate massive oppositions in the personality. This is the power of palm reading, to show every dimension of our personalities.

Remember, any ulnar loop is ignored – you are only looking for patterns other than ulnar loops and whenever you find one, it's a powerful character trait.

Now let's look at the meaning of the most common variations of print patterns. The mirror finger is the one most likely to show a radial loop and the first digit to examine. Some patterns are very, very rare; for instance, you will never see a tented arch on the antenna digit. Only the most common variants are listed here.

MIRROR FINGER'S PRINT PATTERN

Whorl
Marked sense of individuality, secretive, single-minded, a need for space. Difficulty in taking orders, happy with own company, prefer to work alone or unsupervised. Eccentric, dislike of crowds. Intelligent, thoughtful, insular, unusual interests and hobbies.

Simple arch
Cautious, stubborn, unpretentious, self-effacing, reliable, loyal, family-orientated. A skilled pair of hands. Emotionally blocked, old-fashioned. Work and security very important. Love of nature and animals. A dog or cat lover.

Radial loop

Hyper-receptive to others, insecure, likely to over-identify with other's needs. A 'people person', super-nice, a carer, though can be touchy as finds criticism unbearable; can't say 'no'. Able to 'tune in' to anyone and connect with them. A flatterer.

Composite

Uncertain about who one is, philosophical, unable to make life decisions, a marked impartiality and diplomacy. Easily persuaded out of a goal or plan. Never certain about who one is and what one wants.

Tented arch

Intense, goes too far, excessive, over the top, fascinated by any form of personal transformation, likes to entertain, teach, or motivate others, needs excitement. Loads of charisma. Never dull, prone to burnout, needs to learn to relax.

THE THUMB'S PRINT PATTERN

Whorl
Acts independently and alone, self motivated, needs to demonstrate independence, innovative and original in approaching new projects. Happy to follow courses of self-development from books, online and alone.

Simple arch
Extremely stubborn, thorough, persistent and practical in approaching tasks, not afraid to get hands dirty. Very unlikely to follow idealistic or innovative investments, or opportunities. Likes to follow well-trodden paths to wealth, self-betterment and diet.

Composite
A two-way mindset, inconsistent, hard to stick to a course of action, a vacillating attitude. One that holds back, but who is able to follow two courses of action at once.

THE WALL FINGER'S PRINT PATTERN

Whorl

Disregards dogma, rules and convention, odd or unusual beliefs and lifestyles. Very likely to follow a spiritual or philosophical path of an alternative culture. Freedom always more important than worldly success. Likely to break out of any parental religion or culture.

Simple arch

Straightforward and pragmatic attitude to work and lifestyle. A serious, secure, well paid job is important. Has a sense of duty and likes order, method and fairness in values. Justice important. Wants a stable lifestyle and traditional religion.

Radial loop

Culture, lifestyle, and values never secure and entirely open. Easily adapts to different lifestyles, careers and other cultures. Usually over-conformist or strongly alternative or both.

Composite

Has a perennial sense of doubt about career, philosophy, values and lifestyle. Likely to follow two part-time careers. Open to all religions, cultures and lifestyles.

THE PEACOCK FINGER'S PRINT PATTERN

Whorl
Individual and original in creativity, dress, music and the arts. Has good spatial awareness and a flair for design and imagery. Likely to express a love of images, visuals. Good at any sport needing skill with speed and timing.

Simple arch
Has a need for physical expression. Likely to love archaic skills and admires traditional art forms and old fashioned iconography. A love of historic and classical ideals of beauty. Repressive, old-fashioned tendency in tastes and dress style.

THE ANTENNA FINGER'S PRINT PATTERN

Whorl

Enjoys 'insider' knowledge and specialized language. Secretive sexually. Endures long periods without intimacy, interspersed with frantically passionate episodes. Drawn to unconventional relationships.

Simple arch

Repressive sexually. Likely to enjoy communicating the basics of language to children and adults in a teaching environment. Reticent about intimacy. Drawn to very masculine or hyper feminine partners.

CHAPTER FIVE

Palmer Patterns

Interpreting the Prints on the Palm

As well as the prints on the fingertips, more than half the people whose hand you read will have one or more prints on the palm as well.

Before we look at the palm prints, we need to understand the various zones of the palm . Whenever you see a line, print or marking on any particular quadrant, the marking can only relate to the part of the palm it's found on.

The quadrants

The palm is split into four unequal quadrants. Each section relates to a different aspect of the primal brain. It's helpful to know about these zones because when we examine the lines and markings on the palm, we'll know what area of human experience they relate to.

We mark out the quadrants with a straight line down the middle of the base of the wall digit to the centre of the palm 'cusp' - the slight depression in the base of the palm. We then find the point where two major lines intersect between the thumb and index finger and draw a straight line from this point to the

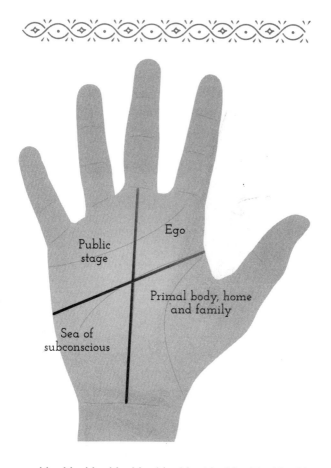

Ego

Public
stage

Primal body, home
and family

Sea of
subconscious

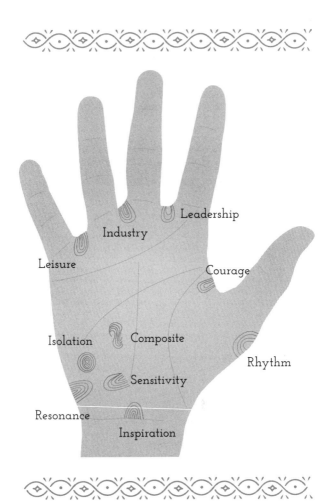

half-way point of the opposite side of the palm. This will create four quadrants.

The four sections of the palm are known as the sea of subconscious; the ego and personal power zone; the public stage area and the primal body, home and family quadrant.

The sea of subconscious is where our collective subconscious is found. Here are your dreams, intuitions, ancestral memories, your deep fears and desires and your spiritual connection.

Above this is the public stage, this is about the need to connect to the wider world of other people, the need for recognition, and for intimacy and sexual connection.

Under the index finger is the ego and personal world where the sense of ambition, ownership, need for power and self-development are found. The area around the thumb rules the body, the family, the home, the need for shelter, children and security.

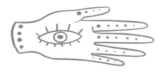

Interdigital loops

The first two palm prints are very common little loops that form at the point where the fingers are joined by a web of skin.

Loop of leisure

This is a loop situated between the peacock and antenna digits. It heightens the pleasure principle and makes one prioritize leisure time. Hobbies, crafts, skills and sports are important. With this sign, escape and holidays come before career.

Loop of industry

Found between the wall and peacock digits, this is the mark of someone who takes work and industry seriously. Career and duty are a kind of pleasure.

Loop of leadership

This is a very rare marking. This loop is found between the mirror and wall digits. It shows a natural organisational ability and the knack of easily acquiring status within a group. A natural manager.

Loop of sensitivity

A loop found around half way up the palm below the peacock or antenna digit. It indicates a heightened psychic ability, a sense of being aware of an undercurrent. Also, it creates sensitivity to danger.

Whorl of isolation

A whorl in the sea of subconscious. This is a signal of someone unreachable in terms of their inner, deeper personality. There's a need to be private and alone a great deal. It's a strongly creative marking, found more often than not on writers and actors.

Loop of resonance

This loop faces outward on the very edge of the palm. It's a sign of high receptivity to the Earth's energies, and a powerful love of the natural world. Always there's a gift for dowsing and healing and a feel for energy points in the body and in the Earth. Usually there's a fascination with mystery, magic and the unknown.

Composite on Sea of Subconscious

This is a very rare marking. It gives constant emotional ups and downs and confusion about deeper feelings. There's always difficulty in maintaining a stable emotional bond and often unstable relationships. The bearer of this marking is fascinated by gender, sexuality and psychology.

Loop of inspiration

Like a fountain of inspiring impressions, this loop rises up from the bottom of the palm. It's common on artists and musicians, spiritual seekers and those fascinated by, and open to, mystical experiences. Dreams are always an area of interest for anyone with this sign.

Loop of rhythm

This is a somewhat squarish type of loop, found on the bottom edge of the primal Home, Body and Family quadrant. It shows a strong sense of rhythm and a love of music. The need to dance and listen to music is deep in the bones of the body.

Loop of courage

A loop in the area just above and near to the thumb is a marker of drive and competitive energy – someone who is physically courageous, who seeks and needs challenges. It's very common on sportspeople and martial artists.

CHAPTER SIX

MAJOR LINES

Major Lines

Let's start with some helpful, introductory points about the major lines:

- There are four major lines and they are by far the most important ones on the palm.

- If a major line is of average length and form, its function is fine and it's not terribly important. It's where a major line is weak or broken or missing, or of an unusual length or form that is interesting to a palmist.

- The major lines slowly change and develop throughout one's lifetime.

You should always read the lines of the palm *after* working through the previous observations of skin texture, print pattern, etc. This will mean you have already established major character traits and the lines are read *in the context of* these qualities.

Always note differences between the active and passive hands. This can highlight contradictions between the developed and latent personalities. Any line that runs all the way across the palm from side

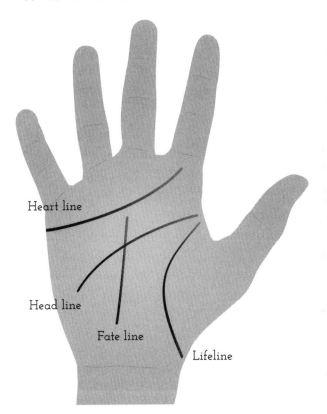

Heart line

Head line

Fate line

Lifeline

to side or top to bottom creates an obsessive, fixed personality.

All major lines start at the same point in the palm but they vary hugely in where they end.

Lines are representative of brain activity. The more lines on the palm, the more complex, highly strung, and active a person's mind is. When the palm is covered with a multitude of lines, the mind is a blizzard of thoughts and mental impulses. When the palm has only a few lines on it, it shows someone lacking psychological complexity but who is highly focused – a 'what you see is what you get' kind of person.

The life line

This line in medieval times was thought to show the length of a person's life. However, this has long been disproved – there are many people in their 90s with short lifelines.

The lifeline in fact shows by its length and strength a person's stability, sense of security, practicality and physical vitality. When the line's short, it shows a rootless, insecure personality who is likely to change home and loyalties quickly and who has little staying power. Weak lifelines are always the sign of someone that will cling to a more stable (and usually more affluent) partner to give them stability. The line represents the gut, so when short or very weak, it will indicate gut and digestive problems. As this line keeps us grounded, those with a short line will tend to be 'off the planet' to some extent; liable to put their faith in angels, auras and unrealistic concepts. There are benefits of the line being short, however, as insecurity will often drive a person to attain wealth, power and influence to compensate.

Ideally, this line is clear and strong, beginning above the thumb and running in a semicircle around the thumb ball to the base of the palm.

Establishing absolutely rigid physical routines of exercise, diet and sleep strengthens a poor lifeline in a matter of months.

If there's a fork at the base of the lifeline, this is known as a travel line, it shows an adventurous spirit and a need to wander the world.

Sometimes the line sweeps very wide around the thumb ball into the centre of the palm. This is a sign of enormous energy and lust for life. The opposite, where the line is almost straight and stays very close to the thumb, shows caution and timidity.

Sometimes this line has a break in it. This shows major life changes, like divorce, family disruption, moving country or health changes. Often the line is stronger after a break, showing a more vital and positive energy after the crisis has passed.

A lifeline that runs from the bottom of the palm with a strong branch reaching up to the edge of the palm below the index finger shows someone obsessed with the perfect body, diet, house and living standards.

Timing on the lifeline

As the lifeline is the most by far consistent line in the palm, it is the only one that can be marked chronologically with any degree of accuracy. The beginning at the top is year zero and the base where the line ends is around 84. Don't make predictions based on markings on the lifeline, as the line may well change by the time the marking is reached. However, it can show in the form of breaks or interruptions

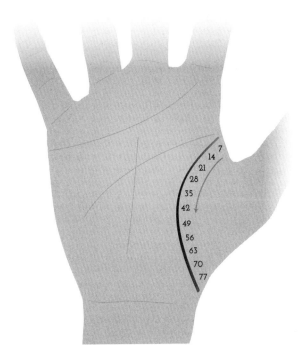

where a person has undergone a major life change.

The head line

The head line shows our mental focus. If the line is fuzzy and full of islands, it shows a cloudy, highly-stressed mentality. If the line is fine, clear and without breaks, it shows laser-like concentration.

The head line starts near or connected to the top of the lifeline. A long head line will end close to the opposite edge of the palm. A short line will end beneath the wall finger. An average length would end under the peacock digit.

When this line's long, there's lots of mental processing going on. Long head lines are found on philosophical people, writers, consultants, speculators, and those that constantly gaze into future possibilities. When the line completely crossed the palm, effectively cutting it in half, this is known as a Sydney line. The Sydney line is associated with high intelligence and great reasoning power, but also dyslexia, compulsive thinking, childhood behavioural difficulties, Attention Deficit Disorder and sleeplessness.

A short line head line shows mental focus only on the here and now. This pattern is easily underestimated, as short head line people are amazingly productive. A mentality that deals only in the real, the concrete and the tangible gets an enormous amount done as they apply everything they know into real-life experiences. This mindset acquires skills and abilities, sets targets and wastes no time on speculation. However, they are not at all far-sighted and don't see the bigger picture as their world view is limited.

Any islands, breaks or fuzzy areas in the head line will destroy mental clarity. However long the line, if it's of poor quality, a person can't focus or think clearly. Poor quality head lines are found on highly stressed, disorganised people who find it hard to think things through. This line is easily strengthened by avoiding stressful situations and by learning to focus the mind on simple, practical tasks – like mindful gardening.

The straightness or angle of the head line is important. If the head line is straight, it shows level-headedness, rationality and a mind that works to a conclusion based on observation, experience and factual knowledge.

The more the head line bends (it always bends downwards) the more the head line dips into the sea of subconscious where the pool of inner perceptions lie. Bent head line people love magic, the mystical and metaphorical. Bent head line people make leaps artistically and are highly imaginative and deeply introspective. When the line is very bent, it can create a introverted and highly subjective personality with a vivid imagination.

How connected or separated the head line is to the lifeline at the beginning is important. This shows the extent of psychological independence. The greater the space between the beginning of the head line and the lifeline, the more aspirational, adventurous and independent the personality. If the gap is a centimetre or more it shows someone confident in their own opinions who's moved a long way from their parents and upbringing psychologically and, usually, physically. A large gap is a highly aspirational sign.

The more the head line stays stuck to the lifeline, the greater the lack of confidence someone has in their own opinions and viewpoints. It suggests very slow maturity and a natural follower. It's often the sign of dominating parents, strict schooling or a deeply religious mindset.

A branch at the end of the headline is known as a 'writer's fork'. It is by no means exclusive to writers,

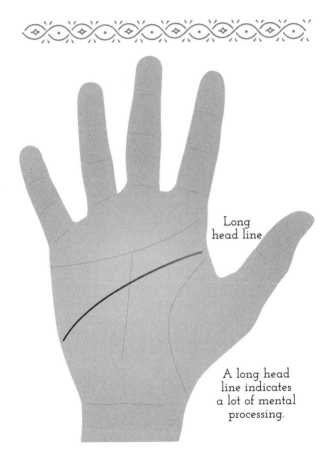

Long
head line

A long head
line indicates
a lot of mental
processing.

however and shows a versatile and inspirational mindset that is good at problem-solving.

Single Traverse Palmer Crease

Rarely (only in 1% of people), you'll see the head line and heart line fuse into a single line. This is known as a Single Traverse Palmer Crease and used to be called, in less enlightened times, the Simian Line. It's the sign of a deeply repressive and obsessive personality. Thought and feeling are fused together so they can't express themselves emotionally and tend to get locked into themselves. People with this line are exceptional in the strength, single-mindedness and focus they bring to whatever they do, to the exception of everything else and this often leads to enormous capabilities. Such people find it hard to accept change in their circumstances and even more difficult to be objective.

People with a Single Traverse Palmer Crease should always be encouraged to relax as there are great inner tensions at work.

The heart line

This line indicates the depth, expression and nature of our emotional responses. Remember, as with any line, it must be read in reference to what you've already found on the palm, especially the skin texture. A coarse-skinned soul will always have dirt under their fingernails, and will never whisper Shakespearian sonnets, however clear, strong and expressive the heart line.

This line begins under the antenna digit and usually ends somewhere between the mirror or wall finger. The more deep, red, and long the line, the more passion, empathy and emotional energy the person has. A long heart line would end very close to the edge of the palm below the index finger. This would show someone who had a long list of friends and who would go a long way in their care and concern for others. This is found on the palms of carers, doctors and therapists. If the line crosses the palm completely from side to side, it shows a compulsion to give and respond to others which often causes problems in

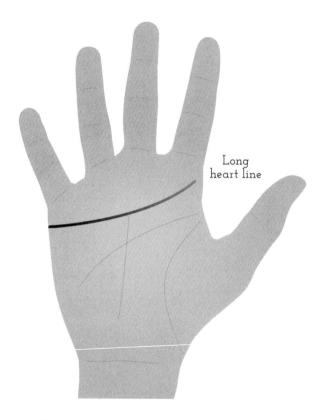

Long
heart line

one-to-one relationships and can lead to emotional burnout.

A short line one would end somewhere under the wall digit and indicates a person who is romantically limited and who has a small circle of friends. Such people rarely range far romantically and can be a little hard of heart. It is often found on those that relate strongly to animals but find people difficult.

A broken-up, messy heart line means a person's somewhat emotionally unstable. Often poor quality lines of emotion are found on enthusiastic drinkers and those suspicious of great emotional outpourings.

Lines which curve upwards close to the fingers are expressive, demonstrative and highly romantic. Probably the ideal point for the line to end is curving up between the mirror and wall fingers.

Heart lines that are straight tend to express emotions through action, practical care, doing favours, or buying gifts. Though not prone to outpourings of emotion, this is a good sign on a parent or long-term partner, where expressiveness is less important than simple nurturing.

Sometimes the heart line splits in two with a higher and lower section - it shows someone operating on two emotional levels. They have a more expressive, social side (the higher, floating section of the line) but there's a deeper, more reticent and limited level of

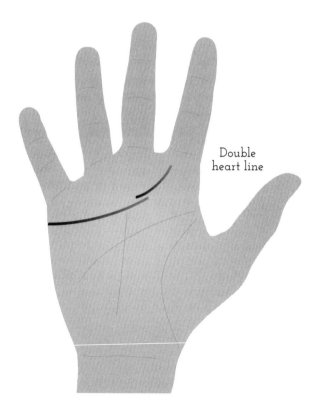

Double
heart line

feeling where they have to withdraw for a while after any intense social interaction.

Jealousy on the palm is easily seen when the ending of the heart line runs down towards or onto the lifeline. This shows emotionally insecurity. People with this marking can't let go.

If the heart line runs up into the mirror digit, it shows high emotional expectations. Such people often worship the object of their affections or are highly drawn to gurus and spiritual beings. If the line curves up into the wall finger, there's an emphasis on family and duty in the affections.

When a series of small lines are seen near the end of the heart line, these are called flirtation lines. This

indicates someone that needs to connect to lots of people of the opposite sex.

The fate line

This line is easily the most difficult major line to identify, as it's so varied in formation. It's often called the 'life path' line as it gives us a sense of character and direction. It's quite normal for this line to be only partially present until a person is in their twenties or early thirties. It can start from somewhere in the middle of the palm, or from the life line, or from within the sea of subconscious area. It always moves vertically up the centre of the palm and ends below the wall digit - this is how you'll recognise it. The fate line shows how clearly your character is defined, and how much energy you put into your personal goals and beliefs.

A long, strong, straight fate line running from the base of the palm up through the middle of the palm shows someone well balanced and straightforward in their dealings with the world. They tend to follow a well defined career path and have a great sense of right and wrong. It shows early maturity and a person with backbone. A straight line will avoid extreme behaviour and will walk a straight path in life.

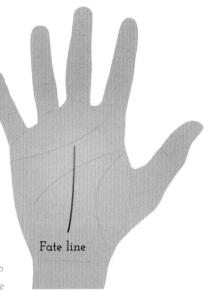

The fate line runs up the centre of the palm toward the middle finger. It may start joined to the lifeline and bend upward or start in bottom left of the palm and curve up towards the middle finger. It may be

Fate line

in fragments, and may be shorter or longer than the illustration. The line always runs towards the middle finger.

A weak, poorly-formed line shows someone who doesn't know who they are and who doesn't know what they want. A weak fate line shows a character only weakly sketched out.

Surprisingly, one benefit of the line being particularly scratchy and weak, is that it's often found on those in a prestigious career. However, they're burning themselves out, striving to attain the glittering heights of other people's ideas of success. It's a poorly formed, fragile life path that cannot be maintained.

If the fate line is straight, the vocational drive is for a conventional career that provides balance between family, social life and personal fulfilment.

If the line starts in the Sea of Subconscious, it marks a personality opposed to traditional values and who wants work and lifestyle that is about working with people, engaging the deeper emotions and who draws on their creativity. Usually a line from the Sea of Subconscious marks a life that is distinctly non 9-5.

When the line begins joined to the lifeline, it indicates a life path based on parental expectation, security, the need to provide for family. This means spending a long time in training and in university. The drive is to work in large companies, corporations and public bodies where security, pension and stability are highly prioritized.

Often the fate line is only present from a point half way up the palm, it shows someone who discovers themselves and their life path mid life and this will always mean major positive life changes. They will always say that at this is when they 'woke up' or first discovered themselves.

Rarely, the fate line runs all the way up the palm, from the very bottom into the base of the wall digit. It shows someone obsessed with work and duty. It creates a fixed, inflexible character who never changes hobbies, work and life choice. Establishing physical goals that are difficult, like running a marathon hugely benefits the fate line.

Always compare the active and passive hands as there is often vastly different fate lines on the passive

hand to that marked on the active. This indicates massive life choice shifts as the person matures.

Breaks, islands, bar lines and duplicates

All the major lines may break and re-form, have an island somewhere along their length, have a short, bar line crossing, or (very rarely) the line is doubled.

A break anywhere on a major line shows a major life change in the energy of that line – in either home, health or family (life line); emotional and love life (heart line) work and direction (fate line) or personality and way of thinking (head line). Ideally after the break, the line becomes deeper and stronger, and this shows that the change has lead to a more positive and fulfilling outcome. If the line becomes weaker, it can mean a little support and counselling is required.

Islands are always signs of confusion and stress. They show a loss of focus and perspective and enormous effort. When an island is seen, a person always needs to de-stress in that area of their life.

Bar lines are where a short line crosses a major line. These indicate obstacles to be overcome. Usually

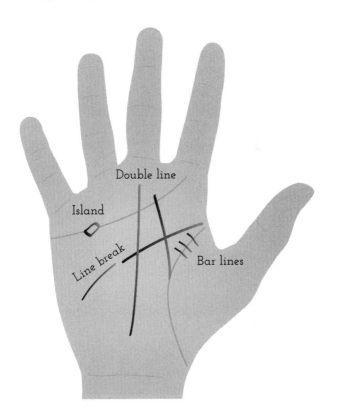

Double line

Island

Line break

Bar lines

these are temporary setbacks, but where there are a series of bar lines, like stitches on a major line, it can show that a new approach is needed.

When a major line is doubled, it shows a double function and two levels of operating. This is a massive advantage, as anyone with a doubled line can shift between two completely different way of functioning, – emotionally, mentally, physically or in terms of their character. This creates a more complex, changeable person. Actors and people with the ability to connect to vastly different people in different ways often have one or more doubled lines.

CHAPTER SEVEN

Minor Lines

The Minor Lines

The minor lines are far fainter and scratchier than the major lines. They vary enormously in their formation and can change very quickly – sometimes in only days or weeks. This means that the minor lines are unique to each individual – you'll find them different on everyone you read for. Always remember it's perfectly normal *not* to see any particular minor line; some people have none at all.

Just like the major lines, whichever hand the minor line shows up the strongest (active or passive) will indicate in which part of that person's life it has the most effect.

Very rarely, you'll see a minor line that's really deep and red and stronger than any of the major lines. This shows a person using up all their energy in some aspect of life, which may make them gifted, but will be detrimental to their health and well-being in the long term.

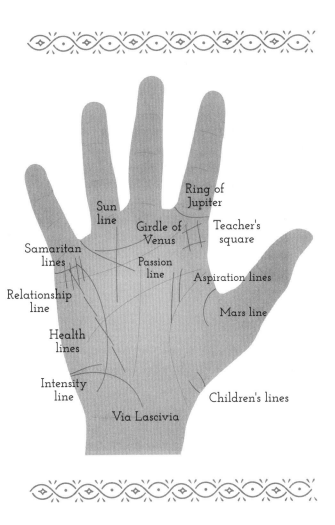

Ring of Jupiter

Sun line

Girdle of Venus

Teacher's square

Samaritan lines

Passion line

Aspiration lines

Relationship line

Mars line

Health lines

Intensity line

Children's lines

Via Lascivia

Sun line

This line is very fine, and runs vertically up to the base of the peacock finger. It's nearly always seen above the heart line so this is dismissed as normal. However, if the line run *below* the heart line for an inch or more, then it's highly significant. This line was once believed to represent fame and someone basking in the sun of popularity. However, its true meaning is of inner joy, a sense of loving privacy and being alone. It's found on those that practice a hobby, art or who do self-development which gives them a sense of inner peace, when they forget the world and lose themselves. Far from needing public attention, those with this line are deeply content without attention from others.

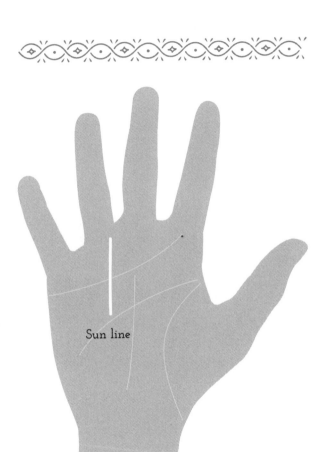

Sun line

Children's lines

Children's lines

One of the most common questions you'll be asked as a palmist is: 'how many children will I have?' Obviously, we have an enormous amount of control over the creation (and prevention) of children, so it's hardly an issue which should be left to fate or chance. When children are marked in the palm, they tend be arise only when the children are actually present in the home and they show up in the home, family and body quadrant (and not on the relationship lines as was previously believed). Children under one's care show up as short, bold lines at the base of the quadrant behind the lifeline on the active hand. Curved lines represent girls and straight lines, boys.

Girdle of Venus

This is a line or series of parallel lines floating above the heart line. This line used to have all sorts of lurid associations, as it was seen as a mark of lechery and decadence. Modern palmists often call this the mirage line as it shows a person wants to be lifted higher into a luxurious, perfect world. It gives a need to escape the mundane, physical world and can easily lead to excessive use of drink or drugs to heighten the emotions. More positively, it gives a sense of wonder, a need to escape, love of the arts and fascination with spirituality, dreams and fantasy. It signals someone unwilling to dwell in the concrete, physical world for too long, but it's always a sign of the love of higher art forms and a sense of refinement.

Whenever this line is found to be very strong, a person is never quite fully present.

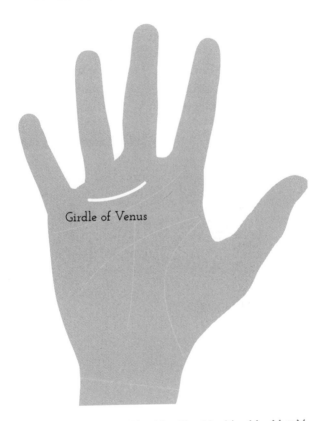

Girdle of Venus

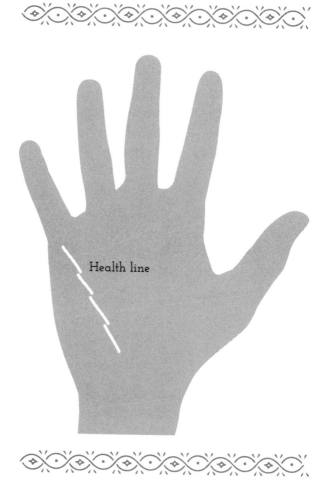

Health line

Health line

Health lines are particularly difficult to identify as they are almost always a series of random, vertical scratchy lines running anywhere from the base of the lifeline to the base of the antenna finger. Sometimes there are four or five fine lines running together, sometimes a sort of ladder effect and, occasionally, just one thin line. There are great implications for health in this line as it's always seen on the elderly and it tends to get stronger as a person gets older.

This line is a reflection of vagus nerve activity and it's strongly associated with digestion, breathing, anxiety and nervous conditions. The more strongly marked the line the more disturbed the stomach acid and digestion and the more the autonomic nervous system is agitated.

In the very rare case when you find one single fine, clear line it shows a very good mind-body connection, a calm, perceptive mind and slow, deep breathing. It's interesting that in good form it's nearly always on long-term yoga and tai-chi practitioners and those that focus on breathing technique. Being sensitive to the diet, digestion and practising deep breathing will clear a messy health line in a matter of weeks.

Intuition line

It's quite easy to get this line confused with the health line as it's in the same area of the palm, but intuition lines are curved, complete and very fine, connecting the deep subconscious area to the base of the antenna digit. This creates a kind of mental phone signal between the intuitive perceptions and the conscious mind. It's common on professional psychics and mediums, and always shows a deep spiritual interest and high levels of awareness.

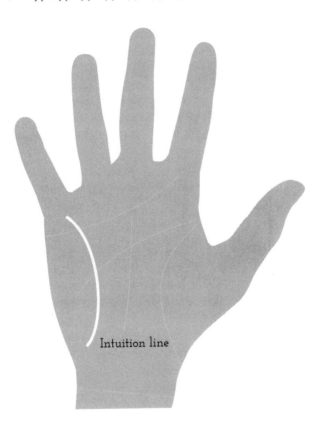

Intuition line

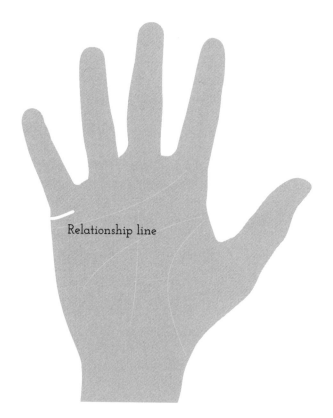

Relationship line

Relationship lines

Relationship lines are found on the outer edge of the palm below the antenna finger and above the heart line. There is a myth that such lines show the number of marriages and children, but this is nonsense. Whether married many times or never, whether nine years old or ninety, almost everyone has one or two of these markings.

In general, these lines can be completely ignored unless they are unusually long, running for an inch or more under the antenna digit.

If the relationship line is long and it curves upward to cut around the base of the antenna digit (the area of intimacy) it prevents trust and acceptance in close relationships and makes a person asexual for as long as the line is present.

If the line is very long and straight, it holds a person back from intimate relationships until they are in their 30's or even later if the line is particularly long.

If a long relationship line plunges downward, crossing the heart line, it shows a fatal attraction to a difficult relationship, this is known as a 'divorce line'.

Passion line

The passion line is a fairly recent discovery which has everyone eagerly examining their lover's palms! It's formed by a line running from the heart line at a 45 degree angle to somewhere near the base of the antenna finger. This line forms a short circuit from the emotions into the sexual area (base of antenna digit). It gives a highly charged sexuality and a fascination with the passionate side of life. Partners are always chosen primarily because of their sexual attractiveness rather than more practical aspects. Those with passion lines are more likely to wander in long-term relationships.

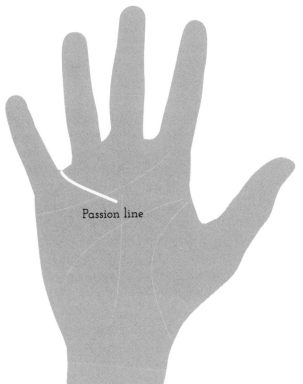

Passion line

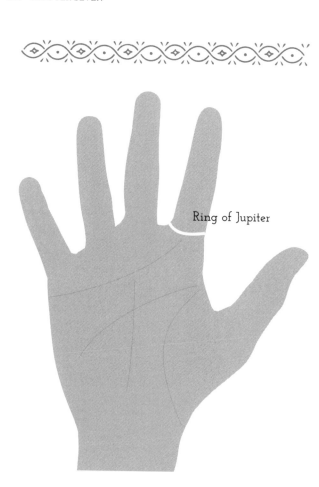

Ring of Jupiter

Ring of Jupiter

This sign is very rarely seen. It forms a semi-circle around the base of the mirror finger. Be careful not to confuse it with the normal crease line always present at the bottom of this digit. Because it cuts off the capacity for self-reflection, it gives great insight into others. It's found on counsellors, psychotherapists, astrologers and you may well develop one yourself, as it's found in abundance on professional palm readers. There's always an interest in psychology when this line is seen.

Teacher's Square

These aren't really true squares, but a formation of four intersecting markings under the mirror finger. This signals the qualities of people management and is a good one to see in a manager or teacher.

Teacher's square

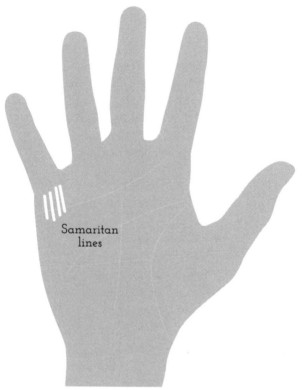

Samaritan
lines

Samaritan lines

These are a series of thin lines running vertically in the area around the base of the antenna digit. They are sometimes known as 'nurses lines' or 'healing stigmata'. Samaritan lines are found on those people that are good neighbours and carers and those with a strong community spirit. There needs to be at least four of these lines to be worth mentioning.

Companion lines

Companion lines are fragile lines found inside the lifeline. Most people have a number of these and they show those close to you in a domestic and familial sense. The passive obviously shows your brothers and sisters and the active your acquired family, life partner or close friends. When there are very many of these lines, they can show a large, complex set of friends and relationships.

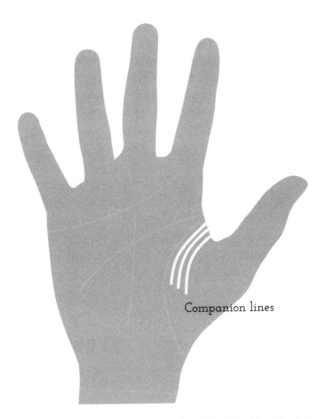

Companion lines

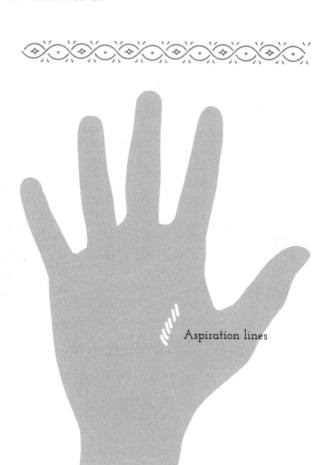

Aspiration lines

Aspiration lines

These take the form of fine, hair-like lines rising up from the Lifeline pointing towards the mirror finger. They are always positive in that they show new 'shoots' of budding enterprises to attain a new job, new child, a bigger house, better situation, positive attitudes and achievements. When you see a series of these (as in the illustration) it shows someone endlessly attending courses and starting new diets and lifestyles.

Mars line

This line is rare, and found within the upper part of the lifeline, close to the thumb. Only if clear and strong and longer than half an inch is it worthy of note – most people have a short, scratchy line here. It's a sign of energy, a competitive nature and the need for challenges. Often those with this sign like to really push themselves physically or are attracted to demanding sports. It's very commonly seen on gym bunnies, athletes, professional footballers and martial artists.

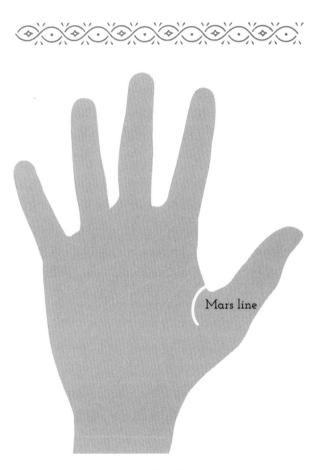

Mars line

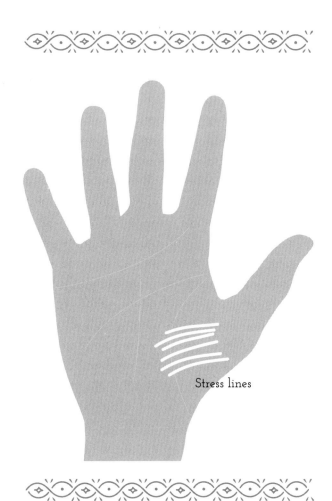

Stress lines

Stress lines

Most people have a couple of fine lines running across the primal home and body quadrant, so ignore these. However, when you see a lot of deep horizontal lines in this area (five or more) it shows too much stress within the home environment and in the general lifestyle.

Intensity line

This line is quite common. It's a delicate, straight line in the sea of subconscious area. It cuts off the deeper, reflective zone of the mind and therefore makes in difficult to relax. People with this line need to seek excitement and movement in order to switch off. Often you'll find this line in parachutists, aerobics instructors, motorcyclists, racing drivers and skiers – they will do anything to stimulate the senses.

Intensity line

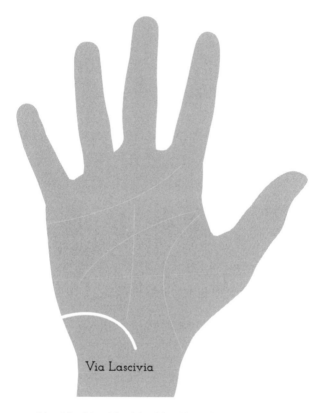

Via Lascivia

Via Lascivia

This line is found in the same place as the intensity line, but it's strongly curved instead of straight and often in a broken-up formation. Often it can run all the way to the lifeline. It shows the immune system is hyper responsive and so the presence of allergies is highly likely. There can also be irrational fears of, for instance, heights or deep water.

Random markings

Part of the ancient baggage of palmistry can mean that people will approach you to interpret the odd cross or star formation, fearing it predicts something ominous. Do reassure anyone who asks that these markings are mostly meaningless. Everyone has the odd squiggle or random cross on their palm. In fact, if they have an over-long index finger or complete crossing head line, that is massively more important!

You can always make a guess at the meaning of a marking from where you find it. If it's on the home, body and family area, for instance, it can only relate to this area of a person's life. Crosses show two opposing energies or drives and the need to make a decision. Stars are a complex of little lines showing many possible options and tend to herald an opportunity. Forks and tridents at the end of any line show a broadening out of potentials and greater capacity to function on different levels. Again, don't get lost in random markings, as they are of little importance and can change very quickly.

CHAPTER EIGHT

How To Give A Palm Reading

Let's Read a Palm!

OK, take a deep breath, we're going to actually read a palm.

First of all, though, some important points.

When you read someone's palm you're working in a caring profession and people are vulnerable to your insights. You can easily say something that will worry and upset your subject so you need to be tactful, sensitive and alert to the words and language you use.

Good advice is to *breathe deeply, speak softly* and *take your time*. Giving a reading can be stressful, because often people's expectations are sky-high. It's common for a client to be certain you'll tell them the name, age and hair colour of the soulmate they haven't yet met and the fact that they once had a cat called Bibi!

You need to explain that you aren't going to make scary predictions – everyone's fate is in their own hands. You are going to outline their deeper personality and reveal aspects of their authentic self they may not be aware of.

The way you read a hand is to work through all the points in the order you learned them in this book. Start with the hand shape, then skin texture, then finger length and so on.

Never rush, wait until you've looked at all aspects of the palm before you start your analysis.

Always examine both hands and note any differences, these are hugely important because they explain contradictory elements in a person's personality.

Bear in mind that every single pattern on the palm has a good and bad aspect. A tiny index (mirror) finger may be lacking in self-esteem and be somewhat self-neglectful, but they will never take themselves too seriously, will not be egoistical and will have some deep drive for display (because by contrast the peacock will be long), perhaps for performing, creating or acting out a role. Look for the good in every issue you raise (while being honest about the negative). Do let your client join in the conversation – when you see a very long mirror finger, you can ask: 'do you fear failure?' 'Was responsibility heaped upon your shoulders at an early age?' and so on, so that the person being read for can feel part of the process and you can get feedback on your perceptions.

Try to see every hand you examine as a lesson for you to learn something.

Never forget that when you look at someone's hand, they are totally exposed. Be kind, be gentle, but always be truthful.

Psychic impressions

You may find intuitive impressions floating up. Palm reading switches on your psychic abilities. This is a positive sign and shows that you're relaxed and getting onto the wavelength of your client. Do tell your client when you get a flash of intuition – but don't under any circumstances go all 'fairground fortuneteller': 'I'm seeing a pink house with a blue door' (this is not terribly important in relation to, for instance, a Single Traverse Palmer Crease and Water-ruled palm – these are massive issues).

People often make enormous breakthroughs in a palm reading. They suddenly see why they've gone for the wrong sort of partner or why they doubted their artistic ability or why they always need to be in control. Huge potential for change emerges when we truly understand ourselves. A good palm reading is like holding up a mirror to someone's soul and there is

enormous power, magic and possibility in the process.

Test Your Skills

OK, no more theory, it's time to put your palmistry abilities into practice. We're going to examine the hands of Katie, a 32 year-old right-handed woman. Look carefully at both her left and right palms (overleaf) and compare them. Do go back to previous chapters to refresh your memory if you need to. Try to respond to the questions as fully as you can from your observations of her palm and put your comments down on a piece of paper. Take your time. When you've worked through all the questions you'll hopefully know an awful lot about Katie – check your comments against the answers at the end of the chapter – you'll be amazed at how much you've learned!

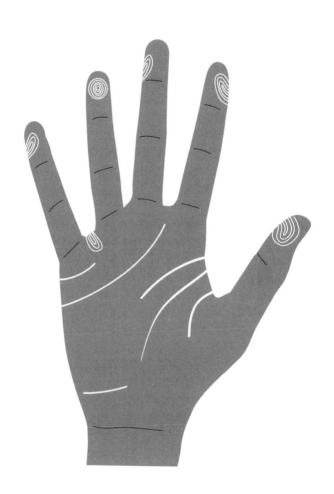

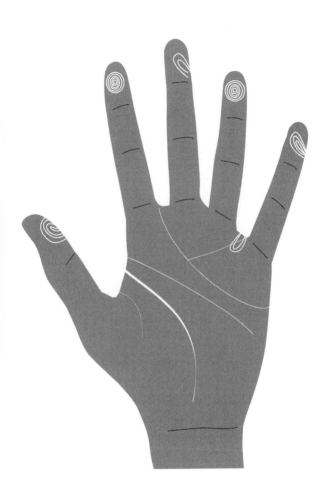

Questions

- What hand shape does Katie have? Is she likely to be an intense, dynamic personality with a competitive nature? What qualities does her hand shape give?

- The skin texture is paper (hard to judge without being able to touch the skin) – what kind of environment would suit her? Is she someone that loves to be outdoors and who is impervious to temperature and weather?

- Let's look at the digits. The mirror finger is the most important – is it long or short or average? What does her mirror finger tell you?

- What about the print on this digit, compare the active with the passive hand. What does this mean?

- Now the wall finger. Is this long or short or average? What about the prints on these digits?

- Now the peacock digit – long or short or average? What does the print patterns on this finger mean?

- Antenna digit next. Long or short or average? Print pattern?

- The thumb next. Long, short or average? Print pattern?

- The fingers and thumb are all stiff and only move a little when you pull against them. What does this tell you?

- Let's look at the lines. Starting with the lifeline – does Katie's lifeline shows she's secure, grounded, stable and has a fixed lifestyle? Any differences from active to passive hands?

- Now the heart line. What can you say about these – is Katie emotionally limited, repressed, or obsessive?

- Now the head line. Is she subjective? Does she have an introverted, inward looking mind? Any significant differences between active and passive head lines?

- Now the fate lines. Is Katie clear about herself and her life direction?

- What minor lines can you see? What do they mean? Any minor line differences between active and passive?

Test print answers

Katie has a rectangular palm with long fingers – therefore these are Water hands. This certainly doesn't give an intense, competitive nature – quite the opposite. Katie is easily shaped and moulded by the people and situations around her. She is highly flexible and adaptable and extremely responsive to the needs of others. The long fingers give a fascination with dreams, intuition, magic, mystery and the arts.

Katie's skin texture is paper. This is fairly common. It creates a responsiveness to visual and verbal stimuli and is quite sensitive; it doesn't make for an outdoors person. Putting the skin type with the hand shape we have someone who is naturally responsive to her surroundings, but who would want to use this energy in a visual, verbal or cerebral way.

Moving onto the mirror fingers, they're very long. This indicates a controlling personality with high

standards. Katie exudes a sense of authority and will find herself in positions with lots of responsibility. She can be bossy and demanding but would never expect more from others than she expects from herself. She's had to grow up very quickly - either from a very pushy mother figure or one who was not able to mother her sufficiently. Katie will not bend to another's will very easily.

The prints patterns are a whorl on the active mirror and a radial loop on the passive. These are polar opposites and show a conflict between her private and public personalities. At work she's highly independent, happy to work alone and loves space. However, in her private life, though still a bit of a control freak (long mirror), with people important to her she's a pleaser and easily loses her sense of herself. In her private life she can be highly defensive, prickly and easily offended (all radial loop qualities).

Now let's look at the wall finger. These are long. This gives a serious attitude to profession, family, and duty. Remember that those with a long wall finger often work in large buildings and institutions, so Katie will find herself in a serious professional environment in a large building with lots of qualifications and grades to attain.

The prints are ulnar loops, so we shall ignore them.

Peacock digit next, obviously these are short in comparison with the mirror. This can limit the extent that Katie will go in order to court popularity and creativity – her pride and integrity (mirror finger) means she won't be strutting her stuff on the stage. However, whorl prints on these digits give originality in creativity, dress, music and the arts, along with good spatial awareness and a flair for design.

The antenna finger is next and it's slightly long. This is always a good feature to see as it shows natural

language skills, wit and eloquence. The prints are ulnar loops, so ignored.

Katie's thumb is of average length and has loops on both, so we're not going to dwell on that. However, both thumbs and fingers are stiff, so she's strong-willed and keeps herself in a tight grip with quite a stiff and inflexible mindset.

Now let's check the major lines. We'll start with the life line. This has the bottom section missing on the active hand and it's even shorter on the passive. This shows a fundamental insecurity, a tendency to move around a lot, a lack of stability and someone who is a little 'off the planet' - prone to fanciful ideas. Combined with the very long mirror finger, this confirms a difficult childhood and that Katie has and is working hard to get on solid ground, financially and practically. It's very likely she'd be attracted to a more fixed and stable partner. On the positive side,

the short life lines will mean Katie can be very quick to grasp new opportunities, and will be highly mobile in pursuit of her ambitions.

The head line next. These are clear and straight on both palms, but the active hand's headline is much longer. The straightness of the lines give a level-headed, rational way of seeing the world. The length difference shows that Katie tends to be incredibly short-sighted in her attitudes passively, and has had a childhood where she applied herself to lots of projects and applied every idea she ever had. On the active side, she's developed a much more reflective, wider world view, so is more considered and less likely to jump straight in with both feet. However, we are building up a picture of a consistent over-achiever here. The headline is separated from the lifeline by a large gap, showing an ambitious and high minded mindset. There is every reason to think that

Katie would move a long way psychologically and physically from her roots.

Now let's look at the heart line. It's clear, curved and ends between the mirror and wall fingers. This indicates an expressive, romantic, and powerful emotional response. This is a great sign for connecting, empathizing, feeling and emoting.

Now the fate line. The fate line is somewhat fragmented and formed from several fine lines. This shows a lack of clarity about goals, direction in work and character. It's likely Katie still hasn't worked out exactly what she wants from life and is likely to have wandered in her direction. Probably her work is one where she has to mould and shape herself to fit the job, rather than the other way around.

Now for the minor lines. There's a long, extended relationship line on the passive hand (much shorter on the active), also an intensity line on both active

and passive hands and a Mars line (much stronger on the passive hand). There's a strong passion line on the active hand.

The extended relationship line makes for a block on intimacy and it would be very difficult to form close relationships for the early part of her adult life. She has no issues as far as lovers are concerned but in terms of serious relationships Katie has trust issues. The Mars line on her passive hand shows a hugely competitive streak and it's very likely, given the intensity lines that Katie would engage in some sport or serious exercise programme. She loves to challenge herself and, though not obvious on first meeting, she would be a formidable opponent in the after-work tennis game. The intensity lines mean she'd have trouble relaxing and would need to have a way of letting off steam in a lively way.

The passion line on the active hand is going to give Katie a sexual, passionate nature and it would be

impossible for attractiveness not to be important in her partnerships.

Katie's palms are typical of anyone you might read for in that they are full of contradictions. She's a responsive, adaptable character, given her water palms, but is bossy and somewhat rigid given her long mirror digits and stiff fingers. She's got strong values and high self-esteem (again the long mirror) but is insecure and quite prickly (short life lines and radial loop on the passive mirror). She is very romantic and sexually highly charged but has problems with intimacy. She is an over-achiever but isn't sure where she's going and what she wants.

Katie's response

Oh my goodness, where did you get all this stuff? Yes, I'm a people person. I'm a Cancerian; is that why I have a Water palm? And yes, I'm highly competitive,

I swam breaststroke for the county of Essex in my teens and still do squash and loads of sporty stuff. My partner, Josh calls me an eager-to-please control freak – yikes, it must be true!

And all that stuff about my mother – she suffered from depression while I was growing up, so I had to fend for myself from primary school onward. I guess I am a high achiever when I think about it; I was deputy head girl at school and got a first at university. I certainly do have a problem with failing. As for career, well, what Johnny said is a bit worrying. I run the Human Resources department for a very large legal company – it involves a good understanding of protocols and employment law, lots of counselling, negotiation and empathy in spades, so doesn't sound too far off my skill set? I guess I did drift into it, and have had a lot of jobs. I was warned by my therapist (yes, I have one) that I'm closer to burnout than I think. Wow! This has given me so much to think about.

Next steps

Now check over all the points raised in Katie's palms and make sure you can see exactly where all the issues are marked. Then take ten sets of prints of people you don't know too well, work through all the points in their palms that stand out and write out a little summary. Go back and check through your five 'rules of thumb' (see page 14) then present your readings to your 'clients'. Once you've got all the feedback from each person, remember that every single reading you do is a lesson for you to learn from. Now you really are on your way to being a serious palmist!

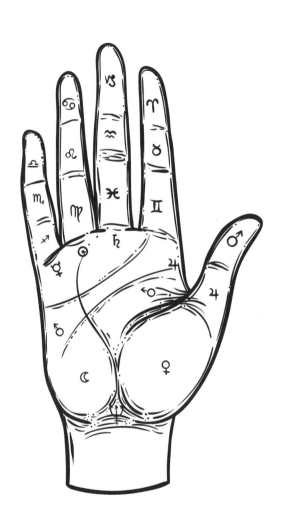

CHAPTER NINE

PALMISTRY AT A PROFESSIONAL LEVEL

Having completed your palmistry journey through this book, perhaps you'd like to take it further and think about becoming a pro? If so, here in this section you'll learn lots of hints and tips to refine your skills to become a high-level, hand-reading hero.

Lifelong Learning

Probably the first and most important point to make is that you need to see each hand you read as a chance to grow. Don't be frightened by what you don't know. No palm reader feels they have the skills and ability to read a hand well at first. Ask questions about features you see on any hand to reinforce your understanding of what any sign means. Get the person whose hand you're reading to clarify and confirm your observations.

So, for instance, when you see a short head line, ask: 'so do you find you tend to put ideas into action quickly, without looking at the bigger picture?' Or ask the person with lots of whorl prints: 'Do you find you need a lot of alone time?' Listen carefully to the answers you get. This sort of enquiry will soften your approach and avoids you having to make serious, definite statements of fact. It will help you to learn from the clients themselves the words and language describing their individual palm patterns, and you can use these same words and ideas in future readings. The path of palmistry is a long one, on which you never really stop learning and growing.

Go gently

When you read someone's palm, you're effectively a form of counsellor, with all the responsiblilities that entails. You can easily say something that will worry and upset your subject. You need to be tactful, and very careful of the way you present information. Don't look disturbed or worried by issues or markings you see in someone's palm. Never bring up traumatic personal issues, like child abuse – unless the client introduces the subject themselves. You may observe, for instance, a very short heart line that only goes half way across the palm – share what you're seeing without specifics. 'There are signs here that you have a lack of trust with your emotions, that you often feel cut off from others and unable to connect to them.' This might be a good way of putting this to your client, then let them share their experience and you can explore the issues together. This is a much more diplomatic and gentle way of looking at an issue rather than blundering in with statements like 'Oh, dear! Terrible heart line! No chance of love for you!' Astonishingly, I have heard a palmist say this to a client at a spiritual fair! So, be tactful, and proceed gently.

Don't give easy answers

As you gain experience in reading hands, you'll inevitably come across people sitting in front of you because they're in some kind of crisis – they've come to you because their partner has deserted them for someone else or they're facing bankruptcy, for instance. It's very tempting to give simple platitudes to reassure them and make them happy, for example: 'Don't worry, I can see a much brighter future ahead, you're going to meet an amazing new partner.' Always remember that your job as a serious reader is not to solve people's problems for them, nor to give fantastical and probably untrue reassurances. You are in the unique position of having an insight into how the situation they're in came about. Maybe the relationship failed because the tiny index (mirror) finger made them lack a sense of power and responsibility in the marriage. The bankruptcy was caused by them having a fire hand with grainy skin so they were prone to push too hard and take risks and so on. The reading you give is a brilliant opportunity for the client to take a good, long, hard look at themselves and to be encouraged to address any issues and change their behaviour. Without your help, people can so easily get trapped in cycles, repeating the same patterns over and over. You hold the key to free them to live better lives.

Point to the power

Often you will find that simply reassuring a client's strong points is enormously healing, particulary where there is a lack of confidence. Someone, for instance, who has a radial loop print, can easily lose self-belief when subjected to criticism. But when they are told they have a gift: how this radial loop gives them the capacity to 'tune in' to other people and be hugely sensitive to the needs of others and that they are a natural healer, this can be a wonderfully powerful boost to their sense of being.

Take the pressure off

Good advice when giving readings is to **be relaxed and slow down.** Giving a reading can be hugely stressful if you see it as a performance and are frightened of not impressing your client. You can't, and will never, know everything and can only work at what you see in the hand in front of you, which is always showing deep and powerful characterstics that are hugely important. It's not a bad idea to explain how much palmistry has changed over the past 50 years and you are about to look very deep into your client's palm and show them their deeper motivations, qualities and abilities. You will see things in them they may be unaware of, and you will see issues that they may have struggled with for years. But you aren't about to give them a list of predictions, instead you'll give them the tools to navigate their lives much more appropriately to their individuality. This may well change their sense of who they are and make life more fulfilling.

Make a reading a two-way process

When giving readings, a great tactic is to resist the temptation to fill all the reading time with your own voice and gabble nervously. A good method is to simply tell the client what you're seeing and let them give you their feedback. This means the client contributes to the reading and feels involved. So, you could say to someone with a short mirror digit: 'This short finger indicates to me that you've not been given the chance to develop real responsibility and a sense of your own power, potential and ambition. You may compensate for this in various ways, but you have a deep sense of not being up to the mark. Tell me, what may have caused you to develop this pattern? What was your mother relationship like?' Now your client is able to join in the conversation and can contribute and, often, can let go of inner hurt and pain – it makes your readings far less stressful and the feedback you get is priceless.

Gender and geography

We live in a time when people are hyper-sensitive about stereotyping, particularly as far as gender is concerned. However, it's vital you have some insight into what is average for sex difference in the palms, because we must know what is likely to be exceptional as far as the hand patterns are concerned.

Men have much higher levels of testosterone than women and though individual levels vary, testosterone in males has a powerful psychological effect on the sense of competitiveness, repression of vulnerability, masking of low self-esteem, and the drive to outperform and to dominate within a peer group. Physically, men's palms are substantially bigger, heavier, with shorter tendons, and stiffer fingers than women. Men's hands are generally broader than women's so the square palm of the Earth and Air elements are very slightly rectangular on women's hands. Women's palms are more likely to have slightly longer thumbs than men, as they have a greater degree of self-control. Also, women's palms (with finer skin and more narrow palms) react more strongly to family dynamics – they are more likely to display a long mirror finger as a result of the mother relationship. Men with a long mirror digit tend to be more obviously bossy and self-important than women with the same pattern. Women are also more likely to have a low-set antenna as there are so many families where the birth father is absent and this affects female hand development more strongly than on a man's hand. Women's palms are much more likely to have silk and paper skin. It's very rare indeed to see coarse skin on a women's palm (1 – 2%) - it's much more common on men (11%). Men have straighter, deeper, clearer major lines in general than women.

As far as geographical area is concerned, Water palms dominate and are the norm in most parts of Asia, particularly in Thailand, Southern India and Nepal. To have a Water palm is, in these parts of the world, perfectly usual.

Earth palms are dominant in China, South America, particularly Peru and Patagonia, in Southern Italy and Portugal, also in any non-industrial, agricultural-based society anywhere.

Fire palms are dominant in the USA and Germany and in any business, military or risk-based, competitive sub-group anywhere.

Air palms dominate in Scandinavian countries, also the Netherlands, and in any academic or university environment.

Timing

Most professional readers allow at least an hour for a reading and then will often re-read their clients palms every couple of years – having the client bring their original set of hand prints along so they can take a fresh set and compare any changes.

As a beginner reader, you may well find you can't fill a whole hour at first, it will take you some time to refine your understanding, develop your skills and elaborate your observations, so 20 minutes is a good starting point. You'll find you'll soon need longer as you get deeper into the palms you examine and have more to say.

Experience is all

A very good place to start gaining experience is with spiritual type fairs, open-air markets and at any kind of festival or social gathering. You won't have time to take a hand print in these situations, this is where a good magnifying glass is vital. You can begin by simply asking only for donations and this will give you a priceless amount of experience and feedback. There really is no short cut to becoming an expert without reading lots of palms.

Working practice

If you decide to become a pro, always take a print of your client's palms, record your readings for your client and always pace yourself, don't do more than four one hour-long readings in any one day. It can be very stressful reading for much more that this as you need to be completely focused and indeed you owe it to your clients to be completely present for them.

Always offer a money-back guarantee to all clients in all circumstances. The information in this book is unknown to many palm readers and is tried-and-tested over thousands of readings. You can have complete confidence if you follow the guidance here that your readings will be of very high standard and accurate. Offering a money-back guarantee will reassure anyone who comes to you that they are in excellent hands (pun intended – haha!) and shows you have confidence in yourself and in your work. In 40 years of reading, I have only had to return my client's cash twice – not because the readings were inaccurate, but because they didn't like my honest (and truthful) comments!

Look for the good

Every single pattern on the palm has good and bad aspects. Even a pattern like a composite print – which makes decision-making extremely difficult and has historically been seen very negatively has a very positive aspect. The composite will be able to see any idea from many angles and from many different points of view. This may be ruinous in a swift-moving, manager role, but may be brilliant in an academic, counsellor or advisor. Every pattern, no matter how difficult it appears, will be very helpful in a particular situation and it's your job to point towards a good way of utilising any pattern that seems to be difficult. A short, broken heart line may not show the prospect of a brilliant love life, but it can be developed with the proper guidance and can be amazing in a role where one has to be extremely unemotive and rational, for instance on the hand of a poker player. Do be honest about negative traits, but always, always find a way of showing the potential strengths.

Blast the inner bias

We as humans all have a certain level of in-built bias. Because we have different hand shapes, skin textures and personal issues, we are naturally prejudiced because we see the world through the prism of our own processes and our own hands. It's crucial you know yourself through a thorough study and understanding of your own hand. Develop a high level of awareness of your own level of sensitivity, confidence, mindset and grounding. You must do this, otherwise you might judge, value and guide your reading subject wrongly.

If you have a Fire palm with grainy skin and a straight head line, you'll have a very direct, rational and action-orientated nature and you will find you try to push people into action, urging them to drive toward goals, achieve success and move quickly into new situations. However, if you have a person with a Water hand in front of you, with silk skin, a dropping head line, and therefore a highly sensitive, introverted and quite possibly spiritually-inclined nature, this would be totally the wrong advice to give. The world of dreams, feelings and the inner, intuitive realm would be where this person should be pointed as this is where they naturally dwell and where their strength lies. So, as a reader, you need to see beyond your own nature in order to understand those very different to yourself. Be aware of how your own inclinations, element and nature can shape your own attitudes.

Try to be always alive to your own psychological patterns that your hands reveal – your short wall digit for instance, should never mean you constantly advise people to rebel, break restrictions and be less inclined to follow the rules – if someone has a long wall finger, that's exactly what they need and want to do! If you have a long antenna, advising someone with a short, low set little finger to write a novel will be poor advice indeed.

Most readers when starting off find that they have a great rapport with and are good readers of clients that have similar hands (and personality traits) to their own, but struggle with palms that are very different in shape and skin to their own. Slowly, this will change as you gain more experience and develop the dialogue and insight into people vastly different to yourself. If you find you're getting very similar types of palms (and people) coming along to see you, it's a sign you're working in too narrow a way and you need to explore other elements, reach out to other types and groups of people and broaden your scope.

Enter your client's world

One of the most powerful techniques in the palm reading manual is the skill of entering the world of your client and to use words, language and observations that fit their particular mindset. This makes a massive impact on your client and ensures you really 'get' them, and know what it's like to live in their shoes.

To make this method work, you need to use as much as possible rich and pointed observations about the way they experience things. So, for example, when you find a client has silk skin, don't just say 'you're very sensitive', give them some everyday examples of how silk-skinned people react to things: 'You must be able to feel the temperature in a room drop by even a degree or two?' 'You must feel it in your system for days if you have just a couple of glasses of wine?' 'When you go to the dentist for a filling, you must feel brutalised afterwards?'

Try saying to the person with coarse skin: 'How difficult it must have been when you've been stuck indoors in an overheated space – how you must pine to be moving around, and be doing something outside.'

To someone with only half a life line, say: 'You must have lived in lots of different places, but it never felt like you were really home, safe and secure in any of them?'

Speaking to the long mirror finger person: 'There have been times in your life when you've had to give up on people or lose friends who were important to you because of your principles.' These kind of comments make an immediate and deep connection to your client – they feel understood and empathized with in a way they've never experienced before.

Don't use the same language and the same delivery for each client, try to use language and ideas related to the individual issues you see on each individual palm.

As analytical dialogue therapists, our style of delivery can be beautifully refined with our understanding of the element, qualities and issues of our clients. People with receptive Water hands respond to intimate emotional support; they'll feel assaulted by a barrage of analytical theory. Ideas and information, however, is great for the Air type hand. Direct, fast and cutting edge sentences and advice are best suited to the Fire type. Earth-handed folk love to be told about family, home and to be reassured of financial security – they like you to be practical and avoid abstracts.

Never hold back in giving lots of examples of the way patterns in the palm manifest in people's lives. Describe everything. Palm reading is about using language, so use the full range of it to the best of your ability.

The gift of seeing

As mentioned on page 158, whether you're intuitive or not, you'll find during your experience of reading palms you'll get psychic impressions floating into your mind. These glimpses into magic are profound and may unnerve you a little at first. Palm reading switches on your psychic abilities when you deeply immerse yourself in a reading and 'forget yourself'. Whenever you get a flash of insight, it's a positive sign. It's very important to handle intuitive flashes in the right way, however, because you can so easily get lost and lose sight of the massively important patterns you're able to see in the hands.

Intuitive impressions add life and colour to a reading, but they should be used only in the precise circumstances of *giving an example of the way an issue manifests from what you observe in their palm*. This is very important. Let me give you an example: you may be looking at the broken life line on the passive hand of a client and you get an intuitive flash of a couple screaming at each other on the stairs of a dark house, and the man running out and slamming the door. This may or may not be very important and may or may not be part of your client's lived experience, but it could be very insightful. The way to handle this is to tell the client exactly what you're doing - 'I see that there is some kind of fracture to your sense of stability while growing up as your life line is broken. This has left a legacy of insecurity. Your home life was seriously disturbed at one point as you were growing up and I'm getting an intuition that this was because your father and mother argued a lot and one day your father just marched out down the stairs and slammed the door, never to return.' Obviously, you may be wrong about this intuition, but you can be absolutely certain about the disruption to that person's sense of security.

Using this method will mean that you are giving *both* your rational, accurate perceptions as well as your intuitive idea. That way, even if your intuition is completely wrong, your observation (about the life

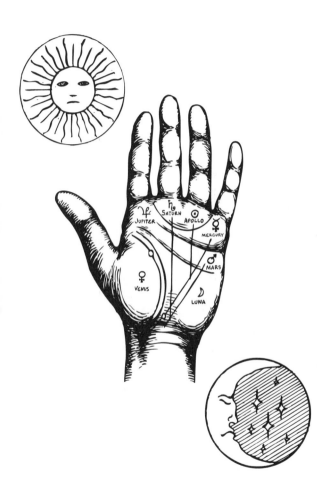

line in this case) certainly isn't. So your psychic side can show images, give you illustrations that flesh out markings in someone's hand, but that's where these insights should remain. It's all too easy to go off on a long ramble of images and ideas on a client – 'I'm seeing a pink house with a high hedge and getting a name, Anna'...'I can see the face of someone with long, dark hair, there's a pain here in my shoulder'. This kind of practice belongs to the realm of the medium, the tea leaf reader or the professional psychic. You are a trained hand reader and your gifts lie in translating what you can see in a person's hand into real, lived experience and describing how a person truly is. This is the greatest gift you can give anyone. The fleeting impressions drawn from your subconscious can be wonderfully powerful if woven into your readings, but keep them on track with what you can see and know from the palm.

People often feel completely 'seen' and make great changes after a good palm reading. They suddenly become aware of the issues that have been holding them back, the burdens of guilt, fear, uncertainty and lack of confidence fall away.

To be a palm reader is a wonderful, enlightening experience. You have the chance to set people free. Now it's time for you to step through the doorway and become one of the gifted, special people that can illuminate with your insight into the darkest recesses of the human psyche...

Quick Reference list

Active and Passive Hands represent the outward, adult, expressed (active) and the inner, childhood, latent (passive) aspects of personality.

Palm Shape
Earth palm - square and short-fingered – down-to-earth, practical and non-academic.

Water palm – narrow rectangular palm with long fingers – flows with emotional energy, adaptable and people-orientated.

Fire palm – rectangular palm with short fingers – hot-blooded, dynamic and goal-orientated.

Air palm – large, square palm with long fingers – high minded, lofty, ideas-orientated

Skin Texture

Silk skin – ultra fine and delicate – extremely sensitive to all stimuli.

Paper skin – quite fine and papery – responsive to visual and verbal stimuli.

Grainy skin – not terribly sensitive, good at sports, busy, active and quick physical responses.

Coarse skin – an outdoors person, very tough and hardy, not sensitive.

The Thumb shows self-control and will power. Long and stiff – huge resources of will, strongly applied. Short and floppy – limited willpower resources, feebly applied.

Mirror (index) Finger – the most important as it shows self-reflection, ego, sense of self and personal power.

Wall (middle) Finger – digit of normality, rules, work, conventions, institutions and family.

Peacock (ring) Finger – the drive for self expression, creativity, kudos, the need to be liked, admired and to be on the public stage in some way.

Antenna (little) Finger – the quality of communication, signal, social, and sexual.

Whorl – marker of independence, originality, love of solitude and ability to work alone.

Simple Arch – highly loyal, repressive, hard working and security conscious.

Tented Arch – excitable, intense, dramatic, needs excitement and rest.

Loop - normal and average, goes with the flow, social, adaptable.

Radial Loop – hyper responsive, drive to please, defensive and vulnerable to losing sense of self in other's needs.

Composite – ability to see both sides of any situation, patterns of doubt and uncertainty, unable to see things in black and white, natural counsellor.

Lifeline – curls around the thumb ball. Shows extent of security, fixity of nature, stability, groundedness and health of the gut.

Head Line – extent of mental focus and clarity, also amount of independence of thought from roots and parents.

Single Traverse Palmer Crease – an unusual bonding of head and heart lines, giving a fixed, intense, highly focused and repressed personality.

Heart Line – quality, amount and depth of empathy, romanticism, ability to emote and expression of feelings.

Fate Line – sense of character, sense of direction, sense of self awareness.

Breaks an interruption in a person's life energy in a certain area (depending on which line it's on)

Islands – a sign of stress and difficulty, where things are unclear.

Bars – an obstacle that blocks one's path in the short term.

Duplicates – a doubled line shows two levels of experience of a line's qualities and energy.

Sun Line – an inner retreat, a sense of loving one's own company, a sense of contentment away from the world.

Children's Lines – deep, short lines marked just inside the base of the lifeline.

Girdle of Venus – fine horizontal lines above the heart line showing the need for higher experience and escape.

Health Line – shows condition of Vagus nerve and capacity for mental calm and inspiration.

Intuition Line – shows connection to intuitive subconscious

Relationship Lines – short lines on edge of palm below antenna finger – ignore unless unusually long.

Passion Line – angular line connecting heart line to base of antenna.

Ring of Jupiter – faint line around base of mirror finger – ability to see into others

Teacher's Square – faint square under mirror finger, showing good management, organising and teaching ability.

Samaritan Lines – vertical fine lines under antenna – indicating kindness and drive to heal and help others.

Companion Lines – fine lines within the lifeline – long-term companions, relatives and relationships.

Aspiration Lines – fine lines running upward off the lifeline – ambitions and yearning to climb higher in life.

Mars Line – short line above thumb and within lifeline – competitive and sporty streak.

Stress Line – lines crossing thumb ball – domestic and physical stress.

Intensity Line – horizontal line in lower base of palm – inability to relax, drive to seek excitement.

Travel lines – branch at base of lifeline showing drive for adventure and travel.

Via Lascivia – curved line at base of palm – indicates allergies and likely over-responsive immune system.

Further reading

Most palmistry books simply repeat the same outdated meanings and references. The following books are well worth reading to deepen your understanding.

Charlotte Wolff *The Hand in Psychological Diagnosis* **Methuen 1951**

Fred Gettings *The Book of the Hand* **Hamlyn 1965**

The Book of Palmistry **Tribune Books 1974 reprinted as** *Palmistry* **Chancellor Press 1993**

Beryl Hutchinson *Your Life in your hands* **Sphere 1967**

Frank Clifford *Palmistry 4 Today* **Schauman & Alter** *Dermatoglyphics in Medical Disorders* **Springer 1976**

David Brandon-Jones *Your Palm, Barometer of Health* **Rider 1985**

Andrew Fitzherbert & Nathaniel Altman
Palmistry - Your Career in Your Hands **Aquarian 1989**

Dr. Eugene Scheimann & Nathaniel Altman *Medical Palmistry - A Doctors Guide to better health through hand analysis* **Aquarian 1989**

Beaven & Brooks *The Nail in Clinical Diagnosis* **Wolfe 1984**

Andrew Fitzherbert *Hand Psychology* **Avery Publishing Group 1989**

Johnny Fincham *The Spellbinding Power of Palmistry* **Green Magic 2005**

Acknowledgements

With grateful thanks to Christopher Jones, Chris Swain, Jo, Jai-Jai, Don, Nita, Lisa, Juan, Cavelle, Kathy, and all the thousands of clients over the years who have taught me so much.